LEAN MISSION

HOW TO ACHIEVE OPTIMAL EFFICIENCY WITH AUTOMATION AND CONTINUOUS PROCESS IMPROVEMENT

Laura Smith Hendrix
MBA, CSSBB

Lean Mission: *How to Achieve Optimal Efficiency with Automation and Continuous Process Improvement*

Copyright © 2022 Laura Hendrix
All rights reserved.

No part of this publication may be reproduced, stored in any retrieval system, or transmitted in any form or by any means, electronic, mechanical, photocopying, recording, scanning, or otherwise, without the prior written permission of the publisher. Requests to the publisher for permission should be addressed to the author at lhendrix@theleanmission.com.

Book cover design by Andy Meaden
Book interior layout by Golden Ratio Book Design
Author photo by Susan Heard Photography, LLC

First Edition
Printed in the United States of America

ISBNs:
979-8-9851514-0-4 (paperback)
979-8-9851514-1-1 (hardcover)
979-8-9851514-2-8 (e-book)

This book is dedicated to my parents, Dr. John Randall Smith (Martha Lambert Smith), who taught me the importance of education and have instilled in me a passion for lifelong learning that is invaluable.

CONTENTS

Acknowledgments xi

Foreword xv

Introduction xix

Match Made in Heaven: Continuous Process Improvement and Robotic Process Automation (RPA) . . . 1
   Background/History 6
   Opportunity Identification for Process Improvement and/or RPA 10
      Prioritization 15

Continuous Process Improvement. 21
   Methodology (DMAIC) 23
   Define 25
      Documentation 25
      Stakeholder Identification and Collaboration – Project Charter. 25
      SIPOC 26
      Current Process Mapping 30
   Measure 32

- Analyze 33
  - Root Cause Analysis 33
  - Brainstorming 33
  - 5 Why's 33
  - Affinity Diagram 34
  - Pareto Chart 35
  - Fishbone Diagram 36
  - GAP Analysis 37
- Improve 40
  - Solution Development 40
    - Solution Brainstorming 40
    - Focusing on Win-win Solutions and Avoiding Win-lose Mentality 40
  - Solution Selection 44
    - Solution Selection Matrix 44
    - Multi-voting 46
    - Implementation Plan 46
    - Communication Plan 47
    - Training Plan 49
    - Monitoring and Control Plan 49
    - Pilot 53
  - Control 56
    - Monitoring Metrics 56
    - Transitioning to Process Owner 56

Robotic Process Automation (RPA) 59
- RPA Center of Excellence (CoE) Steering Team 59

- Software 62
  - Licenses 63
    - License Types 63
      - a. Studio/Development 63
      - b. Attended Robot 64
      - c. Unattended Robot 65
    - Licensing Model 65
  - Orchestrator Management 66
    - Orchestrator Accesses 67
    - Run Logs 69
- Infrastructure 72
  - Servers 72
- Access Provisioning and Storage 73
  - Accesses 73
  - Credential Security 74
- Roles and Responsibilities 76
- Team Model 77
  - Building Your Team 77
  - Inhouse vs. Contracted 79
- Process 81
  - Policies and Procedures 81
  - Assess and Prioritize 82
  - Process Definition Document (PDD) 86
    - PDD Creation 86
    - PDD Reviews 87
  - Development 88
    - PDD Handoff 88

- Solution Design Document (SDD) 89
- Development and Best Practices 89
- Automation Code Storage 91
- Migration to Production........................ 92
  - Migration Plans and Methods 93
- Hypercare..95
- Maintenance.....................................96
  - Incident Management and Reporting............96
  - Monitoring....................................96
  - Production Troubleshooting 97
- Business Continuity – Backup Plans and Communication................................ 99
- Control and Management 100
  - Standardization 100
  - Folder Structure 107
  - Program Reviews............................109
  - GAP Analysis 111
  - Reporting................................115
  - Continued Stakeholder Involvement..........117
  - Citizen Developers..........................119
    - a. Risk Classification 120
    - b. Citizen Developer Policies and Procedures ..120
- Collaboration: IT Infrastructure and Change Notification 122
- Importance of Communication....................126
- Growth and Strategic Planning 132
- Transitions and Change..........................134

Conclusion 143

Appendix 145
  Frequently Asked Questions. 145
  Managing Resistance to Change. 170
    Resistance to Standardization .175
  Reference Tools and Resources. .179
    Templates 179
    Resources 187

ACKNOWLEDGMENTS

THERE HAVE BEEN SO many people who have helped me gain knowledge and experience along my journey. I feel certain that I will leave some out of these acknowledgements, and my sincere apologies if I have left you out. It has taken a village to give me the opportunities I've had to learn and gain ever-increasing experience in the fields of process improvement and RPA.

First, this book would never have been written without the encouragement to write from Blake Mendrop, P.E., Principal Owner — Mendrop Engineering Resources, LLC. When I was working in civil engineering for Blake, he asked me to write — first letters to a mayor to summarize site plan reviews and then Response for Proposals (RFPs). As English was my least favorite subject in school and I didn't enjoy writing, I told Blake that I couldn't write. He told me that anyone who could talk as much as I did could put the words on paper. Thank you, Blake! I now love writing.

Thank you, FedEx! I greatly appreciate all those I worked for and with at FedEx. The list could extend literally around the globe. The training and experience I received at FedEx have been invaluable. To Mr. Fred Smith who had the vision for the FedEx Quality Driven Management (QDM) program and drove that initiative from the very top, making it a huge success — "Thank you, Mr. Smith!" (Incidentally, I always referred to Mr. Smith as Mr. Smith and was often corrected that everyone calls him Fred. The day I meet Mr. Smith in person, and he asks me to call him Fred, I will. Until then, it's a very respectful Mr. Smith.) Thank you to Rosanne Forgione, one of my former managing directors and now a friend, from whom I learned so much. Many thanks to Kinei Lin, also one of my former managing directors, who was responsible for my receiving the prestigious FedEx Five Star Award.

Thank you, First Horizon Bank! I was recruited in 2018 to help them create the vision that their EVP-Operations, Amy Shreve, had to stand up both a process improvement program and RPA in Operations. Thank you, Amy, for entrusting your vision to me! We did it and went on to be promoted as the enterprise programs post-merger with IBERIABANK. In 2018, Amy's vision was unique. Now, most enterprises see the value of combining these programs in some way to benefit from the synergy between them.

Many thanks to Anthony Restel, President, Regional Bank at First Horizon Bank, and Randy Bryan, Chief Transformation Officer (CTO) of First Horizon Bank. Anthony and Randy recognized the value of the process improvement and RPA programs that had been stood up in

Operations and promoted me to lead these programs at the enterprise level post-merger with IBERIABANK. Thank you, Anthony and Randy, for entrusting these programs to me at the enterprise level and for your continued support helping ensure the success of these programs!

Thank you, Bryan Jordan, CEO of First Horizon Bank! In 2019, Bryan spoke to Operations and told the employees he wanted to hear from them. Soon after, Bryan set up a call time and gave out his number. Many leaders say things like this but don't really mean it. Bryan did mean it and continues to listen to employees at the bank as everyone strives to best serve the customers. As First Horizon Bank moves toward the changes that will be required due to the pending acquisition by TD Bank, I know that Bryan will do his best for not only the bank's stockholders but also its customers and employees.

Many thanks to my Harvard Business Analytics Program (HBAP) colleagues who served as beta readers for this book. Thank you, Glenn Hopper, Renee Bourbeau, Aileen Weiss, Cynthia Conway, and Scott Suckow! When we were going through the HBAP program, we learned so much together. The community we have built post-program, continuing to support one another, has been invaluable. A special thanks to Glenn Hopper for writing the foreword to this book.

On a personal level, I would like to thank my husband, Bill, as well as my children, John, Brian, and Katie, who have not only accepted my propensity to be focused on doing the best job that I can for my employers but have also admired that trait. My younger sister, Clara, has been an inspiration to me my entire life. Having suffered from partial paralysis since 8 months of age, she has not only endured a lifetime of challenges but is happy and thankful each day. Her indomitable spirit has inspired me to try and be everything I can be. Many thanks to my sister, Jennie, who encouraged me to explore robotic automation.

I have been blessed to have had many people that have loved me and encouraged me in my life. A special thanks to the McClard family, Jean, Bill and Cynthia, lifelong family friends who loved me even before I was born and have continued to love me my entire life.

Disclaimer: Any program that challenges the status quo, changing existing processes, is going to run into resistance and issues. Any of the challenges mentioned in this book should not be considered unique to the enterprises where I have worked. I learned that they are indeed universal to most enterprises and should be expected. Our role and purpose in providing efficiency improvements is not to point out flaws or criticize — it is to recognize the inevitable challenges we will face and to work collaboratively with everyone involved to create win-win solutions that will be the best for our enterprise as a whole.

FOREWORD

ENCAPSULATING THE WORK REQUIRED for a digital transformation is hard. Developing a playbook that is broad enough to be used by a wide range of businesses across industries, but specific enough to be meaningful to each requires a depth of understanding and experience unique to those who've spent years in the transformation space.

As someone who's spent a career in start-up focused corporate finance, I have lived through this struggle time and time again over the last two decades. I've experienced first-hand the difficulties in improving processes and laying the groundwork for businesses to scale — and looking back, I would have loved some kind of lodestar to follow.

Laura Hendrix delivers just such a guide here.

But even more impressively, her guide is not just a "one and done" transformation exercise. Rather, it is an original approach to managing and driving continuous change. I love this technique because it's more reflective of the reality that a "digital transformation" is not a singular event. The process of transforming is more of an evolution that happens gradually and continuously – just as Laura describes it.

In my book, *Deep Finance,* I outline the importance of defining and documenting processes before starting an automation project. Laura takes this to the next level by explaining how automation and process improvement are a matched pair that feeds equally on both essential components.

This succinct guidebook clearly lays out the path to combine Continuous Process Improvement and Robotic Process Automation (RPA) to gain exponential increases in efficiency. One of my favorite aspects of the book is the way it maps the process and includes a toolbox of solutions and mechanisms for each step along the way.

Laura deftly incorporates stories of the struggles and challenges she has overcome in the course of leading transformations throughout her career, and even includes personal sanity tips such as how to incorporate box breathing into your professional life to avoid blowing a gasket ... which for those of us in the trenches of transformation is likely a near daily risk!

She weaves all these stories throughout the narrative like case studies that make the textbook approaches to continuous improvement seem more human and accessible.

I smiled as I typed that last sentence – thinking back to when I first met Laura in a study group during our time in the Harvard Business Analytics Program (HBAP). I'm not sure how many case studies were included in that curriculum, but it was enough that we both came out of HBAP undaunted by the challenge of writing our own experiences with business transformations including the book you now hold in your hands along with my own treatise on the topic.

In this book, I hear Laura's genuine voice and approach that I knew from the classroom, but I also see the knowledge she has gained in a career spent focused on process improvement and automation. The text is as well organized as her classroom answers were each time she was cold called in Aldrich Hall. Further though, it is clear in her orchestration of such a complex topic that she is in her element and following the greatest adage ever given to aspiring writers, "Write what you know."

Laura has indeed written what she knows and has done so in a clear, understandable, approachable, and human way of which we, the lucky readers, are the beneficiaries.

–Glenn Hopper
Author of *Deep Finance: Corporate Finance in the Information Age*
Chief Financial Officer, Sandline Global

INTRODUCTION

WE ARE LIVING IN unprecedented times. The world of work has and is changing so quickly that it's difficult to keep up. However, we are expected to quickly adapt to our new way of life and beyond that — to thrive. In response, we are not only adapting but we are thriving — doing more with less and redesigning the way we work to become more efficient. The improvements to efficiency not only improve the bottom line for enterprises but also improve the customer and employee experience.

Employees who formerly resisted change may embrace these efficiency improvements more quickly as they realize that time savings not only go back to the enterprise's bottom line but also enable them personally to meet the increasing demands on their time due to personal and family commitments. As the world adapted to new demands during the pandemic, many employees needed the time freed up by efficiency gains to perform additional tasks, perhaps when covering colleagues' sick leave, when home schooling children, or when taking care of sick family and friends. These difficult times and the challenges they brought helped us understand at a deeper level the essential but hard to measure benefit of achieving optimal efficiency: the positive impact it has on people, their families, and their lives each and every day.

As we continue to progress through digital transformation and create efficiencies, you may be called upon to chart uncharted waters quickly while helping ensure security isn't breached *and* that those who don't want to change understand that they must. That is, they must if they want to thrive, and if they want themselves, their coworkers, and their enterprise to survive. Even if these efficiency improvements are not requested by your enterprise, many enterprises will increasingly value those that are the drivers of change and efficiency gains.

Those unwilling to change will indeed end up changing in the worst possible way. They will be forced out, perhaps suddenly, as they become obsolete or the enterprises they are part of fail because they are unable to compete.

If none of this sounds familiar and isn't ringing a bell, this book may not be for you. This book is for those who are being asked to be progressive and create programs that may keep their enterprises in the game — or those who recognize the need to improve their organization's efficiency and are willing to be the trailblazers. This book is also for those who are interested in process improvement and haven't yet been tasked with that responsibility. That's how I started. You may as well.

This will be an exciting, challenging, and at times frustrating journey but in the end, it will be extremely rewarding. When your enterprise is called upon to provide quick assistance to customers during unforeseeable challenges, you will be able to meet the challenge. Indeed, your efforts will not only serve your individual career aspirations but will or should be oriented to helping others; otherwise, you are limiting the scope of your influence. Your efforts *can* help humanity, as some experienced during the pandemic.

By contrast, if you only want to help yourself, it's hard to conceive how you will be successful in the endeavor of optimizing efficiency as this is a team play requiring the assistance and cooperation of a vast number of stakeholders with varying viewpoints. It's essential to value these viewpoints and be the facilitator who finds the best combination of ideas to stand up highly successful continuous LEAN process improvement and RPA programs. The ability to listen and negotiate highly charged waters to achieve the optimal outcome will enable you to stand up highly successful programs. If you haven't started, now is a great time to begin that journey.

I remember when I first became intrigued by process improvement and efficiency. I was in graduate school, and we were asked to read *The Goal* by Eliyahu M. Goldratt, Jeff Cox, et al. Although it was specifically about LEAN and continuous process improvement, it caused me to start thinking more about productivity and all the factors that contribute to maximizing productivity.

I was hooked. At the time, I owned my own small business – a retail shop specializing in antiques and decorative accessories. Not exactly corporate size processes but I had control of them, and I began to improve them. This focus continued in my roles that followed, first focusing on my own desk in my career as a civil engineer and as the opportunities arose, branching out to global process improvement at FedEx and on to First Horizon Bank where I established the enterprise process improvement and Robotic Process Automation (RPA) programs.

Wherever you are in your journey, I encourage you to pursue process improvement and RPA if your interest is peaked by these topics. If you tend to want to constantly improve processes, then you've probably been bit by the same bug I was. You will likely continue to want to improve processes whether it's your desk, your home, or an entire enterprise that is impacted.

As my journey continued, I expanded my knowledge by taking training whenever I could in LEAN, Six Sigma process improvement, Agile, RPA, and so on. I encourage you to never stop learning and pursuing knowledge. There is always more to learn, which brings me to this book. Having trained many employees in process improvement, waste identification, and standing up enterprise RPA and continuous process improvement programs, I began to feel that I could help others learn from my experience.

What can I provide others that will be useful to them? This is the question I asked myself as I wrote this book. *What would have helped me along the way?*

My answers to these questions guided me. The challenges faced while standing up any new program are numerous: where to start, how to prioritize, how to standardize and institutionalize, how to handle change management, how to approach documentation, and so on.

If you work in a highly regulated environment, there are additional requirements added to that long list, and the challenges become even more daunting. If you don't work in a highly regulated environment, you may still want to adopt some of the measures put in place to guard against "the unhappy path." Why? Because when your enterprise starts experiencing success, it becomes tempting to those who are looking for an easy way to gain, i.e., theft and fraud, even if you're a small business.

So where do we start? Well, I am a very visual person and I love methodology. Give me a list, a roadmap, a system for achievement, then stay out of the way. For me, it was these lists and a system for achievement that were missing when I started. I needed a roadmap, a plan, and there wasn't one.

That was my most daunting task — creating a roadmap that would drive success. Without one, the initiatives were continuous efforts in finding our way to success. With that knowledge, my focus for this book was to provide the roadmap or plan I wish I had when going through this program stand-up process, like where do I start? How do I proceed? How do I prioritize, standardize, monitor, and grow?

As I walked through these many questions, I wanted to capture the challenges and thoughts that went along with them as they happened. Every day was an opportunity to learn as in many instances, we were managing unpredictable events. So, I have provided insight into the many facets involved in continuous process improvement and RPA.

As the word "continuous" implies, process improvement is never-ending. We continuously strive to improve every day. We are a work in progress — never stopping, never complete. We are in pursuit of excellence.

Since you have picked up this book or downloaded it, you have most likely either started down this path or are considering starting process improvement and/or RPA programs. It has become your mission.

There are many definitions of the word "mission," but we can understand it as:

"A SPECIAL ASSIGNMENT GIVEN TO A PERSON OR GROUP"

"THE TASK, TOGETHER WITH THE PURPOSE, THAT CLEARLY INDICATES THE ACTION TO BE TAKEN AND THE REASON THEREFORE."[1]

Are you ready to begin your mission?

If so, welcome! This will be an exciting adventure! I hope you are excited to face the challenges knowing that the end vision is so rewarding. Enjoy the challenges as they come, knowing that both you and your team will grow and learn from them.

---

[1] https://www.thefreedictionary.com/mission

MATCH MADE IN HEAVEN:

CONTINUOUS PROCESS IMPROVEMENT AND ROBOTIC PROCESS AUTOMATION (RPA)

WHEN I FIRST BECAME interested in continuous process improvement, it was long before the advent of RPA. At the time, there was a constant trade-off between accuracy and speed. If you wanted improved accuracy, it took longer. If you wanted improved speed, you sacrificed accuracy, i.e., haste makes waste.

Enter RPA. With automation, you could increase speed and accuracy at the same time. Bye-bye trade-off! Who doesn't want faster delivery with improved accuracy? Surprisingly, there are those who don't.

Some people are accustomed to doing processes the way they've done them for years. They understand the manual processes. Many employees are change-resistant and do not want process improvement. They want to keep doing their work as they've always done it. They don't understand how they will work with automation, how they will oversee the automation, and how they personally will fit in if an automation is doing part of the work – even if that automation will alleviate inefficiencies.

But what causes inefficiencies to become embedded into processes? Many processes have grown organically. They started out at Point A, then added Point B, then Point C, then Point D etc. Over time, these processes sometimes grow organically to a point where they are extremely inefficient. In many cases, the more inefficient they become, the harder the process is to understand and improve. Nobody has taken the time to review the process from end to end and purposefully design it to be more efficient.

Now enter the ability to automate. If you automate an inefficient process, you will complete the process faster but will not optimize the overall efficiency of the process and could end up producing a real fast mess.

So, what should you do if you're asked to automate an inefficient process? There are several different options you can take, and the option you choose will depend on your unique situation.

You can delay automation until the processes have been thoroughly reviewed and improved. You can automate to provide immediate lift and simultaneously review the process for a longer lead time improvement. Or you can automate the inefficient process and forget about addressing comprehensive process improvements.

You may choose to take any of these paths based on the process and immediate lift needs versus long-term improvements. This is where decisions must be made according to your team's bandwidth and your enterprise's goals. It's a balancing act and one that you will continuously need to navigate.

While combining the tools of LEAN process improvement and RPA is a match made in heaven, many "matches made in heaven" require work and nurturing. You will need to pay attention to your prioritizations to achieve optimal success.

Remind yourself, your team, and any stakeholders to not let best get in the way of better! There are many times when trying to obtain the best process and best solution means you never actually complete any improvement. Often, the best solutions take so much time and effort that they never get completed. If you're faced with opportunities that may take longer than desired for improvement, work toward incremental improvements instead. Slow and steady wins the race. Perfect may not be achievable in the immediate future, so work on better until best can be achieved.

For example, during a meeting about an automation that my RPA team was developing, I had a manager question me about the fact that we were automating the back end of a process that we were also working on improving end to end. She questioned why we were automating a broken process.

Quite simply, the employees needed an immediate lift while we worked on the process improvement. We had recently gone through a merger of equals and were quickly approaching the conversion of systems and transition from one bank's systems to the others. It was effectively going to double the volume of transactions that some teams would be processing. They needed help and we were able to provide it in the short run while working toward end-to-end process improvement in the long run.

Previously, the RPA team's guidelines were to not automate a broken process or one that was likely to change in the next 12–18 months or that the system was likely to change in that period, but those guidelines went out the door. They didn't apply to our current situation, and we had to adapt. We needed to revise both our guidelines and our goal strategy. We became more focused on providing lift in the areas needed even if it was just for the short term. We were able to provide lift to ensure that the employees didn't become overwhelmed and that our customers received the best service possible.

If you ever must adapt in this way, you may find that there are those who don't understand. They may not be near enough to the team or the work that is pushing employees under water. You can only do your best to explain. Ultimately, these decisions belong to management, and if management wants the help and assistance to be provided, that is what you will need to do.

In our case, both the RPA and process improvement provided a synergy that helped the enterprise, its employees, and its customers by enabling a better understanding of processes, ultimately leading to process improvements, improved efficiency, and better customer service.

However, there are times when the improvements that need to be made are not obvious. You don't know what you don't know until you get into a process and learn more about it. If you encounter these type situations, others may wonder why you didn't do the final improvements needed in the very beginning. It is helpful to remind them that the intricacies and details of some processes are not obvious until you dig into the process more deeply.

As much as we would all like a crystal ball that would allow us to view the entirety of processes instantaneously and know the return on investment (ROI) ahead of time, this is often not the case. An understanding by management and executives regarding the potential for both continuous process improvement and automation and their proactive support is critical to the success of this match made in heaven and is discussed in more detail later in the book.

BACKGROUND/HISTORY

What is LEAN continuous process improvement?

You probably understand continuous process improvement. However, you have probably never thought about the need for process improvement to be a well-planned, proactive part of your enterprise. Many times, processes just evolve into what they are, and proactive initiatives to examine processes end-to-end are never initiated.

If a process is examined or reviewed, people often wonder who thought the way it's done is a good idea. It's important to remember a process may not have started out as it is now. It evolved. When additional steps were added, they were tacked on, and the entire process was not reviewed end to end.

As part of your LEAN mission, you will need to change this habit. You should create a new and better habit for your enterprise to periodically schedule the review of processes to determine whether they are optimal and how they can be improved.

But first, let's talk more about LEAN. What is LEAN, you might be wondering? Well, LEAN is the elimination of waste. Waste comes in many forms. There is an acronym often used to remember the different types of waste called TIM WOODS, meaning:

Transportation – Moving objects from one location to another

Inventory – Holding excess physical products for longer than necessary

Motion – Walking, bending, etc., during processing

Waiting – For parts, approvals, etc.

Over-production – Producing more parts than are needed, such as weekly reports when only monthly are needed

Over-processing – Having unnecessarily high standards

Defects – Reworking to correct errors

Skills – Underutilized capabilities, lack of training, etc.

Through my years of working in LEAN continuous improvement and adding in RPA, I have included additional categories in the acronym as shown in red to help identify areas of waste:

Manual

Repetitive

Transportation – Moving objects from one location to another

Inventory – Holding excess physical products for longer than necessary

Motion – Walking, bending, etc., during processing

Paper, printing

Waiting – For parts, approvals, etc.

Over-production – Producing more parts than are needed, such as weekly reports when only monthly are needed

O – Over-processing – Having unnecessarily high standards

Defects – Reworking to correct errors

Skills – Underutilized capabilities, lack of training, etc.

If you recognize that your processes are manual and repetitive, these are prime opportunities for automation. Also, in today's digital world, the need for paper and printing is in most cases obsolete unless hard copies are required for regulatory reasons. When you see paper in use, ask yourself:

- Why is it in use?
- Is it necessary to comply with regulatory requirements?
- If not, how can it be eliminated?

The cost of paper goes far beyond the paper itself. There are costs associated with ink, printers, and storage, and ultimately the paper must be securely destroyed at some point, i.e., shredded. Usually, where there is paper, you will also see motion, i.e., walking to the printer, storing in filing cabinets, walking to the shredder, etc.

Identifying obvious areas of improvement, such as the use of paper, are opportunities that we call "low-hanging fruit." In the next chapter, we'll start identifying opportunities for improvement. The best place to start is with the low-hanging fruit. These are the easiest to identify and the quickest and most straightforward to improve.

But how do you get started on this journey? Where do you begin? These are the questions I'm frequently asked. Once you or your enterprise has determined the strategic goal of improving efficiency, where and how do you start practically?

OPPORTUNITY IDENTIFICATION FOR PROCESS IMPROVEMENT AND/OR RPA

Let's dig right in. It's important to start identifying opportunities for efficiency improvements. The best way to do that is to start brainstorming.

Where do you start identifying opportunities? A good place to start is simply documenting your list of processes. Every team has processes. Every department has processes.

Make a list of the departments and/or teams you would like to talk to first. Then schedule meetings or calls with them to start discussing and listing processes that seem unwieldy or are current pain points. Which processes drive them crazy?

As you go through this exercise of brainstorming potential areas and opportunities of improvement, it will not only help you start lists but also spur thoughts of similar processes. In addition, it will help you and your team start thinking in a LEAN manner, i.e., questioning how processes are accomplished and whether there is waste and opportunity for improvement. You may find that excitement grows as others begin to envision and understand the improvements that can be made.

To track and document your findings, you can use a spreadsheet like the example given here. This will become a living document that you use and update regularly.

Eventually you may move to other means of tracking such as SharePoint or software designed specifically for this purpose, but this is a good start to get you on the road to achieving efficiency improvements as quickly as possible.

First, list all the processes that your team or the team you're guiding performs and add a description.

PRIORITY (HIGH/ MEDIUM/ LOW)	PROCESS NAME	DESCRIPTION	LEAN WASTE TYPE	VOLUME (HIGH/ LOW)	PROCESS IMPROVEMENT OPPORTUNITY (YES/NO)	AUTOMATION OPPORTUNITY (YES/NO)	COMMENTS
High	Posting Tickets	Tickets are posted throughout the business day using paper tickets. The initiating employee writes a paper ticket, and a manager must approve. The ticket is then walked to another employee who processes the ticket by entering it into the system. The processed tickets are then taken to another employee who files the processed ticket.	Manual, Repetitive, Motion, Printing, Waiting	High	Yes	Yes	Are approvals actually needed prior to processing or can levels be set that do not require approvals? Manual processing needs to be eliminated via RPA.

Many of my colleagues will be shuddering at my recommendation to create a spreadsheet. "No, no, no!" They scream. "We must get away from spreadsheets. They are archaic."

Folks! You must crawl before you walk. Walk before you run.

There is still value in using simple tools to get through your maturity stages more easily. Work in your spreadsheet and once it feels stabilized to you, transition to SharePoint, a database, or software designed specifically for this purpose. For now, a spreadsheet is a good place to get on the road to efficiency improvements as quickly as possible. So, crawl and strengthen your knowledge of processes and opportunities to move progressively to your maturity. You'll get there one step at a time. Plus, planning and gaining experience with these simpler tools within the context of your unique environment will save you time in the future.

The next step is to decide whether a process should go straight to automation or undergo process improvement. Here, strongly consider process re-design prior to automation for automations that involve many employees. For example in one of my roles, there was a process that ~200 employees used where the request came in either by non-standardized email from other internal departments or by calls. We reviewed the front-end portion of the process and determined that forms could be used. This enabled the requests to be received in a standard format, triggering the automation, which processed the request prior to back-end employee involvement. In some cases, it eliminated back-end employee involvement all together. This process improvement hugely improved the customer and employee experience.

Once you've decided whether the opportunities should be addressed with process improvement or automation, use the following layout to add more in-depth information. Create two separate spreadsheets here: one for tracking the opportunities for process improvement and another for the opportunities for automation.

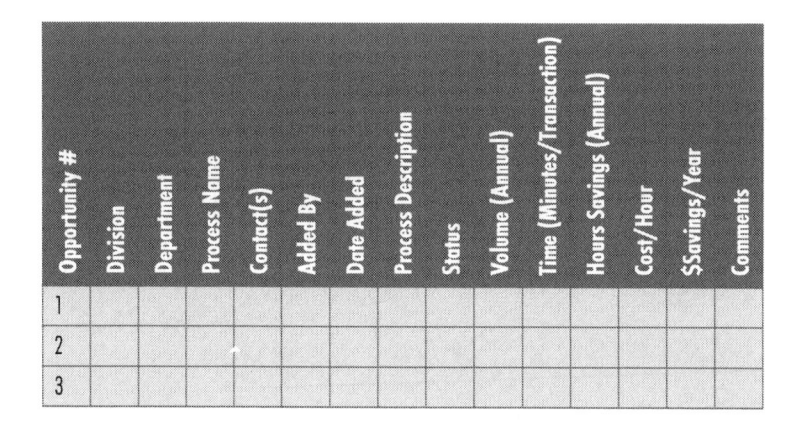

Opportunity #	Division	Department	Process Name	Contact(s)	Added By	Date Added	Process Description	Status	Volume (Annual)	Time (Minutes/Transaction)	Hours Savings (Annual)	Cost/Hour	$Savings/Year	Comments
1														
2														
3														

Now, you will have three tracking spreadsheets. The first is the initial opportunities assessment tracker where you decide whether the opportunity should be managed as a process improvement or automation opportunity. You then have two separate trackers: one for RPA opportunities and one for process improvement opportunities.

For the Cost/Hour column, you can get an average for the level of employees who perform the processes either from management in that area or finance. Be sure to include whatever percentage your company adds for benefits cost. This can be as high as 25%. $ Savings/Year is then a simple calculation ($ Savings /Year=Hour Savings (Annual) X Cost/Hour).

In the chapters on continuous process improvement, you will learn about the methodology used to work through the different stages of process improvement. This process is called DMAIC (Define, Measure, Analyze, Improve, Control). For the spreadsheet for process improvements, the status dropdown options may be:

- Opportunity Identified
- Define
- Measure
- Analyze
- Improve
- Control
- Not Pursued (You will most likely identify some opportunities initially that you will decide not to pursue.)

These status distinctions will become much clearer as you learn about DMAIC.

For the spreadsheet for automation opportunities, the status dropdown options may be:

- Opportunity Identified
- Assess
- Process Definition Document (PDD)
- Development
- Production
- Not Pursued

These categories will also become clearer in the RPA chapters. For now, the opportunities will just be marked as "Opportunity Identified."

PRIORITIZATION

Once you have your initial lists, look closely at the processes with high volume. What are your additional prioritization criteria? If you already know your criteria, great. You're one step ahead. Make additional columns on your spreadsheets so you'll also document the areas of importance and strategic goals for your enterprise.

These may include error prevention, penalty and fee avoidance, customer experience improvement, employee experience improvement, capacity creation, etc.

Customer and employee experience improvement can be very difficult to quantify. However, these factors are important and should also be noted in your list of opportunities. You should be able to absorb some of these improvements into your programs and still have very attractive return on investment (ROI). Some companies make the mistake of only considering opportunities with easily quantifiable ROI, neglecting the harder to measure financial and long-term impacts of error prevention, fee and penalty avoidance, improved customer/employee experience and capacity creation.

When prioritizing, I like to consider the Total Economic Impact (TEI), which includes these areas of consideration:

- ROI
- Error prevention
- Fee and penalty avoidance
- Customer experience improvement
- Employee experience improvement
- Capacity creation

Capacity creation is a huge potential factor when prioritizing either for automation or process improvement. As such, it's also important to consider anticipated volume growth. Wait, what do I mean by anticipated volume growth, and why did I mention that?

Areas that have the highest volume today may not have the highest volume in the future as other areas grow. Having an eye on anticipated volume growth areas can help your company be proactive in planning for and absorbing increased volume without an equal increase in labor costs, as shown here:

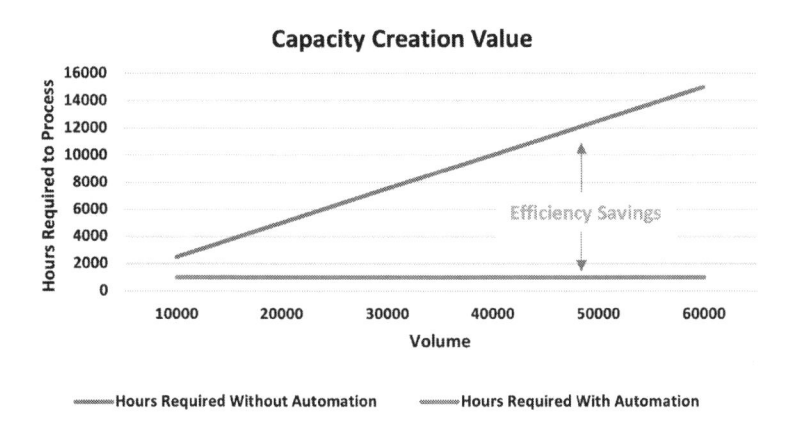

Capacity Creation Value

[Chart: X-axis "Volume" from 10000 to 60000; Y-axis "Hours Required to Process" from 0 to 16000. Upward-sloping line labeled "Hours Required Without Automation" and flat line labeled "Hours Required With Automation". Arrow between them labeled "Efficiency Savings".]

The difference between the trajectory without automation/process improvement and with it is the difference in time required to process different volumes of transaction. Without automation/process improvement, the amount of time and investment needed to process it would increase relative to the increased volume. The time savings that can be realized with automation/process improvement directly translate to the increased profit your company will realize in the future from capacity creation.

Next, you will need to start prioritizing, i.e., deciding which will you approach first, second, third, etc. When we first started making our list of opportunities, we were quite frankly at a loss for how to proceed. So, we did the best we could and got started. We titled Column A Priority.

We used numbers for the opportunities we knew we wanted to go ahead and pursue, i.e., 1, 2, 3...

The rest we put in buckets such as 10, 20, 30, 50, and 99. There were multiple rows/opportunities in each of the buckets. For us, you didn't want to be in bucket 99. That bucket was the one we didn't feel we should ever approach with process improvement or automation.

Why would we place an opportunity in that bucket? In some cases, we discovered that the process was going to become obsolete soon due to system replacement or some other change was needed prior to automation or process improvement.

Priority	Opportunity #	Division	Department	Process Name	Contact(s)	Added By	Date Added	Process Description	Status	Volume (Annual)	Time (Minutes/Transaction)	Hours Savings (Annual)	Cost/Hour	$Savings/Year	Comments
1	1														
2	2														
3	3														
4															
Bucket 10															
Bucket 20															
Bucket 30															

This numbered bucket system became complicated over time as we also identified our processes by sequential numbers, so we had to keep increasing our bucket numbers not to conflict with our numbering system. As our program matured, we completely dropped the prioritization column as our status column transitioned to show our prioritization. For RPA, when the opportunity started progressing through the pipeline, the status changed from Opportunity Identified to Assess, then to Process Definition Document (PDD), Development, and lastly Production. For process improvement initiatives, they moved from Opportunity Identified to Define, Measure, Analyze, Improve, and lastly to Control.

It's much simpler to use the statuses in your spreadsheets to move the opportunities identified through prioritization and completion. But I have provided the bucketing system example in case you prefer it when starting.

You may be hesitant to start this documentation due to the fear of not doing it "right." However, there is no "right" or "wrong" way. The goal is to start and continuously improve your own process.

It's helpful to first focus on high ROI areas. After all, monetary investment is being made to achieve automation/process improvements. The executives committing funding to these investments want and need visible, measurable results.

At this point, you're just trying to do a high-level prioritization, so don't get too hung up on exact numbers and get lost in the weeds. Later, you should tighten up these numbers as your program grows and becomes an integral part of cost savings and earnings reporting. It will happen. Don't get bogged down in that level of detail now though. If you do, you may never get started.

It's also important to remember that executive decisions and their priorities may shift, causing re-prioritization for your team. This should not come as a surprise, but some employees may become frustrated with the shifts in prioritization. You can see this as an opportunity to help them learn to expect and adapt to shifts in company goals and internal politics.

CONTINUOUS PROCESS IMPROVEMENT

NOW YOU HAVE STARTED your list and prioritized, what comes next? It's time to start diving deeper into understanding the processes you have prioritized. This means spending time with the subject matter experts for those processes.

Don't make the mistake of not taking into consideration that employees that know the processes best have other obligations for daily processing. Certain times may be busier than others for them. Other time factors include scheduled vacations, not just for those you need to meet with but also considering their colleagues' vacation schedules as they may be doing double work while their colleague is out, which is not a good time to meet.

My recommendation is to go ahead and start scheduling time to do deeper dives. At the beginning, start with 2–5 opportunities. If the scheduling is challenging for certain teams, you may be able to fill the gaps with the others you have identified.

Keep in mind that on closer examination, you will discover reasons that the opportunities you originally identified and prioritized are not good candidates or not at this time. Some of the factors that may be identified are planned system/platform changes, process changes, or elimination of processes the original interviewee was not aware of etc. If these obstacles are encountered, these opportunities can be moved to Not Pursued.

METHODOLOGY (DMAIC)

Continuous process improvement involves constant change. However, change is difficult for most people — even those who initiate change as part of their jobs. Change is more palatable when initiated by individuals themselves. When it's initiated by others, it can cause discomfort or even anger and resentment.

Understanding and accepting resistance to change will be helpful to you. It's also useful to follow a model that is tried and proven for working through continuous process improvement initiatives. One such model is the model used by those practicing Six Sigma. It is called DMAIC – Define, Measure, Analyze, Improve, Control.

Some enterprises have created their own versions of this process. At FedEx, the process is called ABLE: Assess, Build, Launch, Evaluate. Come up with your own acronym if you like. Whatever the model is called, it's a circular process. Once a process is improved and stabilized, management may want to improve it further for increased ROI, further decrease in errors, and so on. The cycle starts over again with the new or revised goals in mind.

The process starts with forming a temporary team to address a specific purpose. One of the most important functions of the process is team facilitation.

The team will need a facilitator. The role of the facilitator is to guide the process properly. The facilitator doesn't need to be a subject matter expert in the area. In fact, at times, it's helpful if the facilitator doesn't know anything about the process. They are there to guide the team, not to provide expertise. If the facilitator has specific expertise in an area, they should try to keep their expertise to themselves and engage others who have the expertise to provide input while they personally remain neutral.

The facilitator should not be prejudiced toward a specific solution. Their role is to guide the team to develop and choose the solution. If the facilitator doesn't remain unbiased, an optimal solution may not be achieved. Let's walk through the steps of the DMAIC method in more detail.

DEFINE

When pursuing process improvement, we start in the Define phase to improve our understanding of the processes.

DOCUMENTATION

Documenting processes not only brings clarity about the process to those not involved regularly with the process, but also can be used as a tool to help improve understanding and fuel discussions during your team's brainstorming sessions. The documentation can also be reviewed to help ensure that all stakeholders are included. In addition, as time lapses after completion, it serves as a go-to resource for the facts and details that may become foggy.

I highly recommend that you err on the side of over-documenting when you are approaching process improvements. As you are involved with innovation and process change, you may find yourself juggling many balls. It can become extremely confusing and frustrating to remember the minutiae and details of each process and circumstance.

STAKEHOLDER IDENTIFICATION AND COLLABORATION – PROJECT CHARTER

As part of a continuous process improvement program, you should identify all stakeholders for the process at the very beginning. I like to use a Project Charter for this. The charter helps you define the issue/process being reviewed during the initiative, what is in scope and out of scope, the list of team members involved, and a strawman timeframe for when you would like to start and complete each phase.

An initial pass at completing the project charter should only take 15–30 minutes, but it's a living document that can be modified and added to as you go through the phases.

For the first draft, try to envision every department or area that may be impacted downstream or provide input upstream. Be inclusive in your planning. Identify your stakeholders and include them as soon as possible. You will often identify additional stakeholders after your first pass, and these should be added to your charter.

There are many free Project Charter templates available on the internet. Spend some time reviewing the free templates available and understanding the components.

Another tool used is the Supplier Input Process Output Customer (SIPOC) diagram.

SIPOC

By documenting a very high-level view of a process using a SIPOC diagram, the process flow not only becomes clearer, but the SIPOC can be useful when identifying stakeholders — those who contribute to the process, those involved in the process, and those who are impacted by the deliverable of the process.

SIPOC diagrams visualize the process by documenting the very basic components of the process. There are basically five areas displayed on a SIPOC diagram:

1. Supplier(s) – The person, team, or system that provides input to a process

2. Input – The information or item added to the process by the supplier

3. Process – The series of steps that convert the input to the output

4. Output – The deliverable of the process

5. Customer – The internal or external person(s) or team(s) who receive or use the deliverable of the process

SUPPLIER(S)	PROCESS	CUSTOMER(S)
(Provides Input Needed For Process)	(Series Of Steps That Convert The Input To The Output)	(Internal Or External)
Stakeholders:	Stakeholders:	Stakeholders:
1. Stakeholder #1	1. Stakeholder #1	1. Stakeholder #1
2. Stakeholder #2	2. Stakeholder #2	2. Stakeholder #2
3. Stakeholder #3	3. Stakeholder #3	3. Stakeholder #3

INPUT ▶ (between Supplier and Process)
OUTPUT ▶ (between Process and Customer)

There are many free SIPOC templates available on the internet. Spend some time reviewing the free templates available and understanding the components now.

It is also good to start saving templates you would like to use in a template folder so that you have them readily available and can start standardizing your own process of continuous process improvement.

Sometimes, it helps to construct the SIPOC on a call/meeting with the initial stakeholders to brainstorm. Alternatively, you can create an initial draft and review in your first launch call with the team to make sure all stakeholders are involved.

At first, you may experience resistance to include all stakeholders in discussions, as the culture of companies is often for groups to work in silos and then push their solution on other stakeholders after the fact.

It is highly likely you will receive resistance from those not included but if you engage stakeholders from the very beginning, listen to them, and incorporate their ideas, you are much more likely to not only get their buy-in to the process improvement but will also gain their assistance in making sure the initiative is successful.

If you encounter resistance to stakeholder inclusion, you may want to ask yourself the following questions.

- Are those resisting being stubborn?

- Do they just want it their way?
- Do they want to have it their way so badly that they are willing to let the initiative fail?

Experience will help you manage these situations and work through them to help ensure all stakeholders are included and that the team is respectful and open to different viewpoints. Studies have shown that diversified companies are more successful companies. The same can be said for diversified teams. Including varying points of views will ultimately lead to better solutions.

My hope is that although this may be uncomfortable for you at the beginning, you will grow to enjoy the improved brainstorming and solutions delivered. Whichever way you determine is the best way to overcome resistance to stakeholder inclusion, it is important to be diplomatic rather than authoritative. Even if you have support from high places to be able to bulldoze, you may not have this same support in the future as organizational structures may frequently change. If you are a bulldozer and the winds of power change, there may be many applauding and pushing to help make sure you no longer have the power.

Links for resources can be found at www.theleanmission.com.

CURRENT PROCESS MAPPING

It is essential to thoroughly understand the current process to determine where there may be inefficiencies and areas that can be improved. One of the best ways to do this is to create a current process map. A process map is a visual graphic representation of the process.

There are software packages that can be used for this purpose. I currently use Visio. If you do not have special software for this purpose, create a process map in Word, PowerPoint, or whatever you have using a combination of shapes, arrows, and text boxes. Don't let not having process mapping software be an excuse for not creating process maps. Be creative. Be resourceful.

An advanced version of a process map is called a Value Stream Map (VSM). Value Stream Maps show the time spent on each step and indicate whether the step is a "value-add" or not. To be a value-add, the step must add something to the deliverable that is considered valuable by the customer.

Examples of value-adds may be deliverables received quicker, improved communication or information availability, etc. Examples of tasks that are not value-adds might include internal reporting, internal approvals, etc.

There are some non-value-adds that cannot be eliminated. These include compliance and regulatory requirements. Customers do not view these efforts as providing value, but they cannot be eliminated.

Search the internet for examples of process maps and value stream maps and become familiar with them and their uses.

Links for resources can be found at
www.theleanmission.com.

MEASURE

In addition to process mapping, it is important to capture current metrics for the process. These metrics provide a starting point for comparison to determine and communicate achievements or lack of.

Some possible current metrics you may want to capture are:

- Transaction volume
- Throughput time per transaction
- Cost/year for process
- Error rate
- Anticipated future growth (This is important so that high-growth areas can be recognized and improved.)

ANALYZE

ROOT CAUSE ANALYSIS

As the team transitions into the analyze stage, it is crucial to perform root cause analysis to determine the true cause of issues or problems in the process. Tools useful for root cause analysis include brainstorming, the 5 Why's, affinity diagrams, Pareto charts, and fishbone diagrams.

BRAINSTORMING

Typically, team discussions start with brainstorming. Start by asking for input about possible causes of a problem. If you are face to face with your team, it is helpful to put each idea of a possible cause on a sticky note. If not face to face, the suggested causes can just be listed in your notes.

5 WHY'S

As mentioned, the 5 Why's can help with root cause analysis. This simply involves digging deeper into areas. However, the number 5 is not a magic number. You may only need to ask why 3 times or as many as 8, etc. The purpose is to determine the deeper cause of issues, not stick to a rigid number of questions.

Let's take a report being late as an example. The 5 Why's may go as follows:

1. Why didn't we send the report on time?

    We didn't have all the data needed.

2. What data didn't we have?

    Department A didn't send their data in time.

3. Why didn't they send their data on time?

    They had some employees out.

4. Why are employees having to send the data?

    That's the way it has always been done.

5. Can we retrieve the data without involving employees?

    Yes, the data is available in the database.

Initially, one might believe the problem lies with Department A. The actual problem is depending on employees to send the data rather than obtaining directly from the database, which would eliminate employee impact on the process. Whenever you hear an answer like, "That's the way it has always been done.", it is a red flag that the process should be questioned further to determine the best solution. Because something has always been done a certain way is not a good enough reason to keep doing it that way. The optimal way to achieve tasks is the goal.

AFFINITY DIAGRAM

Once the team can't think of any further possible causes, group the causes into similar types, i.e., technology issue, training issue, manual errors (fat fingering, transposing errors, etc.).

This can be easily achieved with an affinity diagram. If you're using sticky notes, start by identifying the categories the causes fall into. Then move all the causes into a category.

This can also be achieved if working virtually by simply moving all causes into a category in Word, OneNote, or whatever platform you are using.

PARETO CHART

A Pareto chart is a useful visual. A Pareto chart is simply a bar chart that is sorted showing the largest to smallest bars left to right, like this:

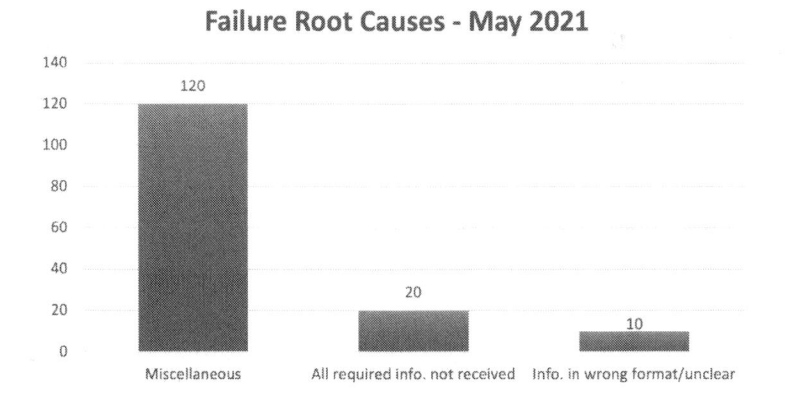

Failure Root Causes - May 2021

Category	Count
Miscellaneous	120
All required info. not received	20
Info. in wrong format/unclear	10

An additional example of a Pareto chart and its use may be found in the Monitoring and Control Plan section.

FISHBONE DIAGRAM

A fishbone or Ishikawa diagram is like a Pareto chart in that it provides a visual representation of causes grouped by category, like this:

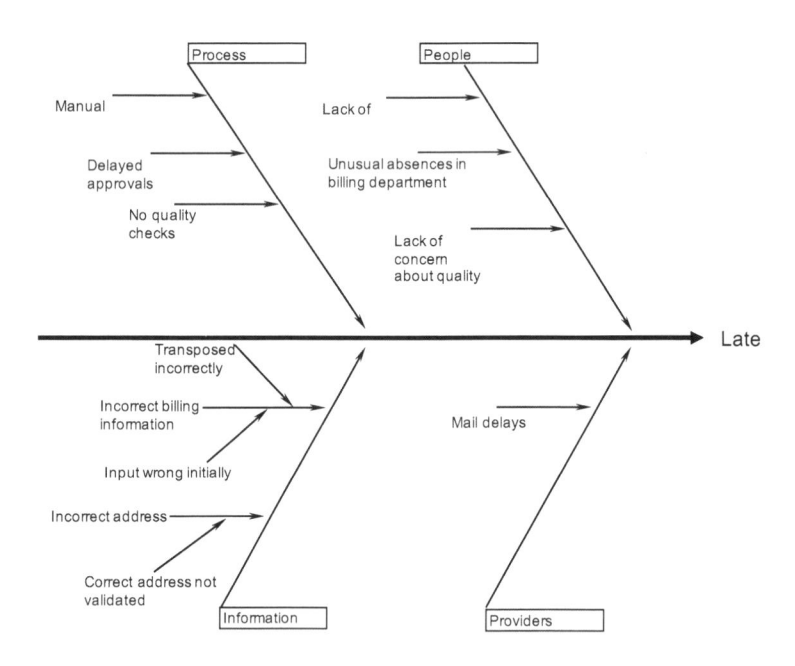

```
                    Process              People
                      |                    |
   Manual ─────→      |    Lack of         |
                      |                    |
   Delayed ─────→     |    Unusual absences in ─────→
   approvals          |    billing department
                      |                    |
        No quality ─────→                  |
        checks              Lack of        |
                            concern        |
                            about quality  |
──────────────────────────────────────────────────────→ Late
              Transposed ↘      ↗                ↗
              incorrectly
         Incorrect billing ──→        Mail delays ─────→
         information
           Input wrong initially ↗
   Incorrect address ─────→
        Correct address not ↗
        validated
                    Information          Providers
```

Using the fishbone diagram combined with the 5 Why's (explained in the next section) can help your team drill down to the root causes and visualize the contributing factors. In a fishbone, as you drill down to the "smaller bones" it is possible to identify the true underlying root causes that should be addressed and the category or categories/areas causing the most issues.

Multiple free templates for fishbone diagrams can be found on the internet by searching fishbone or Ishikawa diagram.

GAP ANALYSIS

Conducting a gap analysis provides clarification on what needs to be done to get from where you are to where you want to be. The first thing is to define the current state.

- How is the process done?
- Who provides input?
- Who performs the process?
- Who receives the deliverable?
- Who are the other stakeholders?

If possible, it is very helpful to conduct a gap analysis in person in a room with a whiteboard, but it can also be done virtually if needed. The important point is to get input from all stakeholders to get as complete a picture as possible.

Once the current state is documented, start discussing what the ideal state would be. Listen to all stakeholders and try to come to a consensus regarding the ideal state. Right now, we are not concerned with what can be done realistically. We want to discuss and determine the *ideal* state.

Next, we discuss the gap between the current state and the ideal state. What are the components of the gap? During the gap discussion, we start defining requirements to get to the ideal state. Gaps are areas that will need to be enhanced/changed to reach the ideal state. The gaps identified may include areas such as technology, training, process re-design, etc. Identify as many as possible.

Now, take each gap identified and discuss how the gap can be closed, the timeframe and resources involved, etc. At the end of this exercise, you should have a clear picture of the measures required to close the gap.

The team now must decide the course they would like to take to start closing the gap. I use the term "start closing" on purpose because it is rarely realistic that the best/ideal solution will be obtained with one effort. The gap closure often must be done in phases. Remember to not let best get in the way of better. Incremental improvements that are more likely to be achieved quickly often provide efficiency improvements sooner than "pie in the sky" initiatives that take longer to get funding and require multiple departments buy-in and resources to implement. (There are various tools that can be used to help the team decide on the solution, which are discussed in the Solution Selection chapter.)

Document your findings well and share them with the team. You may find the documented gap analysis very helpful as time passes and you revisit gap closure and move through the phases.

Research the tools listed in this chapter such as brainstorming, affinity diagram, Pareto chart, fishbone diagram, 5 Why's, and gap analysis and become familiar with them.

Links for resources can be found at
www.theleanmission.com.

IMPROVE

SOLUTION DEVELOPMENT

Solution Brainstorming

Once the team has identified the areas that need to be addressed, the team will need to start developing solution options. A good start is to ask your team for ideas. It is very helpful to tell the team before you start that initially the goal is to elicit and list ideas. It is counterproductive to debate each idea as they are suggested. If you do not prevent this type of debate during the brainstorming, it can thwart the free flow of ideas as participants may become intimidated and not want to contribute their creative ideas. This type safe brainstorming session can bring out much better outcomes than if one contingency is allowed to take over and effectively "bully" their own idea through the process.

Make a list of all the solution ideas that are presented. Ultimately, your solution may be a combination of ideas.

Focusing on Win-win Solutions and Avoiding Win-lose Mentality

Next, you will need to guide the discussion on each solution and the pros and cons. Remember that the facilitator must be unbiased and should not push their own opinion or ideas. These discussions can often turn into criticism sessions if care is not taken. Try to help the team stay open-minded and listen to others' opinions and ideas respectfully.

Some of the differences between facilitating and managing are included here, so keep these in mind when facilitating process improvement initiatives:

FACILITATOR VERSUS MANAGER	
FACILITATOR	**MANAGER**
Not subject matter expert (SME) of process	Subject matter expert (SME) of process
Non-opinionated regarding solution	Often opinionated regarding solution
Does not direct how process should be done — engages stakeholders to determine	Often directs how something should be done
Has higher level focus for all stakeholders	Often has narrow, silo focus on their own team or department

Guide the team to look for win-win solutions. When the team tries to focus on finding win-win solutions rather than on their individual goals and initiatives, better solutions are developed. If the team or individuals aren't guided away from a win-lose mentality, it can lead to win-lose solutions, dissension among team members, and less-than-optimal results. If you see this start to happen in discussions, ask the adamant opposing party whether they see any positive factors in the other suggestions. Sometimes, they will continue to be stubborn and just say no. In these cases, ensure that they remain respectful during discussions and advise the team that there will be an opportunity to vote for the solution the team would like to pursue.

If everyone involved can approach opposing views with respect and show thoughtful consideration of others' views, it can lead to better outcomes for all involved. I had this happen when I was pursuing approval for the use of some software needed by contractors who were providing automation monitoring services. The dashboards they used were built on software we did not use. In addition, there was an initiative by IT to decrease the various numbers of platforms used across the enterprise, particularly if multiple software was being used that provided the same features.

I knew that if we didn't use the contractor's preferred platform, it was going to delay onboarding and cause extra work for both my team and the contractors, but I tried to be a team player and focus on IT's goal. I asked IT what platforms were preferred, presented these to the contractors, and asked if they could possibly work with one of the existing platforms. I then went back to IT and told them the one we could use. It would cause extra time and delays, but we could use the existing platform to support their efforts.

IT requested a call to discuss. Frankly, I was frustrated by yet another delay as this had been in discussion for weeks and it was difficult to understand why we needed to discuss it further. I had capitulated and was adjusting to their requests. What happened was a great surprise.

As IT asked questions and learned more about the software we had originally requested, the tides turned drastically, and they decided that the platform requested was better and more cost-effective than the one they were using. They decided to transition their existing platform to the one we had requested rather than the other way around.

Be patient. This type of turnaround doesn't always happen but being willing to listen and adjust your own agenda can lead to better relationships and better outcomes for the enterprise/business as a whole.

SOLUTION SELECTION

SOLUTION SELECTION MATRIX

If you have multiple solution options, which often happens, the team will need to decide which option or options to initiate. It is often helpful to have a systematic method to determine the solution to use rather than just discussing them. One way to do this is to create a Solution Selection Matrix.

A Solution Selection Matrix includes the various factors of the solutions and weights the factors to come up with a quantitative number for comparison purposes. For instance, some of the factors that may impact solution selection are processing time improvement, error reduction, employee experience improvement, and customer experience improvement.

List the factors the team identifies as important and their weight importance, i.e., 1 = low importance, 5 = high importance. Then give each option a number between 1 and 10 on how well they resolve that category (1 = low). Multiply the rating by the weight to determine the weighted score. Then add up all the weighted scores to come up with the total weighted score for each option.

This is how a spreadsheet might look for solution selection:

	Weight	OPTION 1	OPTION 1 (Weighted)	OPTION 2	OPTION 2 (Weighted)	OPTION 3	OPTION 3 (Weighted)
Improvement in processing time	4	6	24	3	12	10	40
Error improvement	5	1	5	8	40	3	15
Employee experience improvement	1	1	1	5	5	1	1
Customer experience improvement	3	9	27	10	30	10	30
Total score			57		87		86

You can clearly see that option 1 is not as attractive as option 2 or 3. Options 2 and 3 are so close that they require further discussion and analysis. Although this example doesn't clearly identify which solution we should use, it has still been a valuable exercise as it has ruled out one possible solution and narrowed the list of options.

Research Solution Selection Matrix on the internet. Find a template that you like and save it to your templates folder.

Links for resources can be found at
www.theleanmission.com.

MULTI-VOTING

Another method for solution selection is multi-voting. In the Solution Selection Matrix example, multi-voting could help you decide which solution should be used from the remaining options. Multi-voting is fairly straightforward and involves multiple rounds of voting by the team to narrow down possibilities. Team members may be allowed only one vote or multiple votes if the choice of options is large.

After tallying, the list is narrowed down, and voting is done again. This is repeated until a single solution is identified.

IMPLEMENTATION PLAN

After the solution is selected, the team needs to create an implementation plan. The basic implementation plan should detail the action steps/tasks needed to implement the solution, the person or people responsible for implementing the task, and the due date for completion for each task.

The main purpose is to document the tasks, responsible parties, and due dates to help ensure a successful implementation.

Implementation plan templates can be found on the internet, or a simple plan can be created in Excel. **NOTE:** You may want to combine your implementation, communication, and training plans (which we'll cover next) into one spreadsheet with separate tabs to make it easier to reference back and forth.

Action	Responsible Party or Parties	Due Date	Status	Comments

Links for resources can be found at www.theleanmission.com.

COMMUNICATION PLAN

It is important that proper communication is conducted with all stakeholders prior to and during implementation. You want to avoid a deer in headlights reaction when the solution is rolled out. "What? No one ever mentioned that to ME!" Leaving stakeholders out of communications is not the best way to start your implementation.

Work with your team to determine the list of stakeholders who need to receive communications. Also list who will communicate, who needs to be responsible for the communication coordination, what will be communicated, when it will be communicated, and how the communication will be delivered. To help you remember these important factors, remember who, what, when, and how.

Finally, track the status and comments in your communication plan. Excel can be used for a simple but effective tracker. The facilitator will guide the process of completing the communication plan and help the team determine the person(s) responsible for each portion. The status of each portion of the communication plan will be reviewed during team meetings. Create your spreadsheet as follows:

Who will deliver? (Person)	Who is the target audience? (People)	Who is responsible coordination? (Person(s))	What will be communicated? (Text) (Can be linked to a separate Word document)	When will it be communicated and how often? (Date/time)	How will it be delivered? (Platform)	Status	Comments
Carol Speaks – Communication Dept.	Call Center Employees	Team Facilitator, Team Communications Lead, Call Center Manager	"On October 15, 2021, a new process will be implemented"	Oct. 1 10:00 AM CT, Oct. 7 10:00 AM CT	Email		

TRAINING PLAN

By this time, your team should have decided whether training will be required. The information needed for the training plan is very similar to the information contained in the communication plan.

The following template can be used to create your spreadsheet:

Who will develop and deliver? (Person)	Who is the target audience? (People)	Who is responsible coordination? (Person (s))	What will be required for training? (Text)	When will it need to be implemented and how often? (Date/time)	How will it be delivered? (Platform)	Status	Comments
Tommy Trainer	Call Center	Team Facilitator and Call Center Manager	On-demand video and Job Aid	On or before Oct. 1 – on-demand indefinitely	Company training platform		

MONITORING AND CONTROL PLAN

In order to help ensure the solution is stable and stays in place and stable, establish a monitoring and control plan for the new process. The monitoring and control plan establishes:

- what will be measured to determine whether the new process is performing as expected
- what the expected or desired goal is
- who will monitor
- how the metrics will be reported
- who the metrics will be reported to

Key Performance Indicators (KPIs) are typically the terminology used for the metrics chosen that will be indicative of the performance for the process.

For example, if a new process is being put into place for handling call center calls, one KPI might be the percentage of calls managed successfully using the new process. The KPI might be expressed mathematically by calls managed successfully via new process divided by total calls received and managed by new process, i.e., 1,000 calls received and managed via new process and 900 managed successfully equal 90%.

Another essential part of the monitoring and control plan is to establish the goal for the KPI to determine whether the process performance is meeting its goal or needs to be analyzed for additional potential improvements. It is helpful to use color coding such as red for "worse than goal" and green for "better than goal". Sometimes, a goal is established initially with the idea that it will progressively be tightened to continuously improve performance.

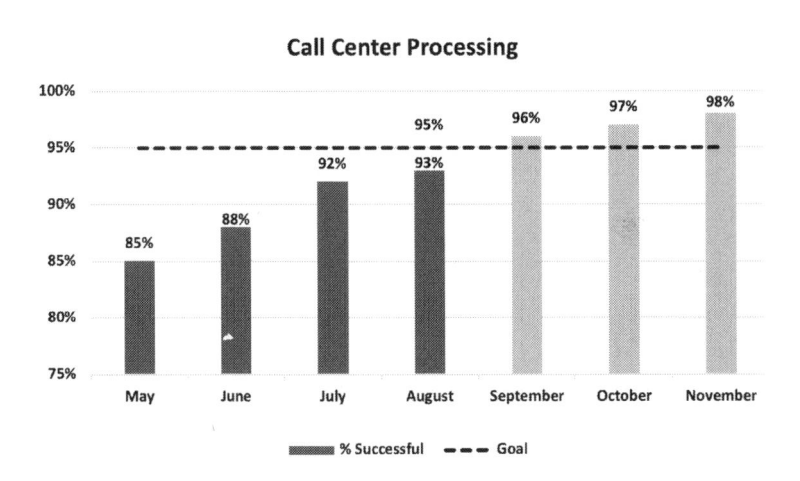

Call Center Processing

Month	% Successful
May	85%
June	88%
July	92%
August	93%
September	95%
October	96%
November	97%
	98%

Goal: 95%

Let's say the initial goal for the metric is 95%. In this example, the performance shown in red is worse than the goal. The control plan would call for additional improvement measures to be reported and analyzed. Once the 95% success rate is achieved consistently, you may want to raise the bar/goal to 98%. In this way, the process will be continuously reviewed, and the performance will be improved.

A Pareto chart for failure reasons would be a good addition to the monitoring and control plan in this case. This shows the root causes of failures listed in magnitude of frequency with the highest frequency shown from left to right.

In this case, the Pareto Chart for May might look as follows:

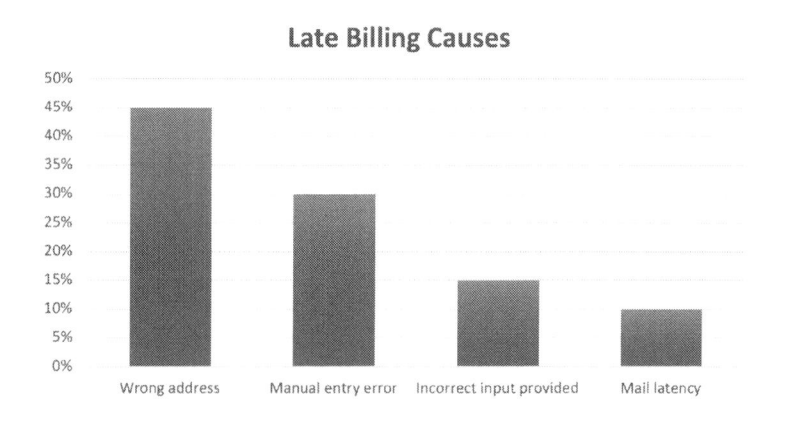

Late Billing Causes

Cause	Percentage
Wrong address	45%
Manual entry error	30%
Incorrect input provided	15%
Mail latency	10%

The most frequent reason for failure in this case is wrong address. The team would need to do a deeper dive to determine the best measures to take to improve in this area. They may also want to research and plan improvements for the other causes shown. Over time, these measures will progressively improve performance.

The monitoring and control plan for this example follows:

Key Performance Indicator (KPI)	Reporting Responsible Party	Reporting Frequency	Distribution Mode	Recipients	Action Items
% Calls Processed Successfully (# Successful/# Total) Goal = 95%	Joe Smith	1 X/ week by COB each Friday	Email	Todd Jenkins, Call Center, and Fred Smith, Solution Architect	Todd and Fred to review root cause Pareto chart to determine whether additional improvements can be made. Periodically review goal and increase when needed.

PILOT

For larger impact initiatives, it is advisable to pilot the solution to a smaller group first to work through and rectify any issues that occur prior to rolling out to the entire group. A pilot is also helpful in validating that the solution is achieving the desired benefit prior to committing to the time and expense of a full roll-out.

First, ask yourself and your team of stakeholders if the initiative is large enough to warrant a pilot. You have involved your stakeholders for a reason. Utilize their expertise and their opinions. Remember, you are the facilitator and not the SME for all the areas involved. Listen! Let this be a team decision.

Let's say the team decides that a pilot is desirable. Enlist the team to decide:

- who the participants should be
- who will be responsible for managing the pilot
- what the pilot should test and achieve
- when the pilot should occur
- where and how the pilot should be conducted

In other words: Who? What? When? Where? How?

In addition, the responsible parties need to be defined. Remember to have a designated party to help you coordinate the pilot team on the business side.

The pilot plan would look as follows:

Who? Pilot Participants	What?	When?	Where?	How?	Responsible Parties
Susie Smith's Call Center team — Carol Jones, Betty Walker, Tom White, Allen Carlisle	Team to use solution for all calls	1/15 – 1/22	In their standard locations	Team to be provisioned access to automation pilot	Fred Smith, Solution Architect, and Susie Smith, Call Center Manager

CONTROL

MONITORING METRICS

Once the solution is fully implemented, the solution will need to continue to be monitored as per the monitoring and control plan. During the initial portion of the implementation, the metrics may not be at the desired goal and there also may be fluctuations. Adequate oversight needs to be ensured during this period to address areas that cause instability and less than desired outcomes.

When the metrics become stable and are at or better than the desired goal, the monitoring and control can and should be passed to the process owner. After all, your team needs to go and help others improve their processes. If you are bogged down by monitoring and control for every process your team implements, your team will not have the bandwidth to pursue additional improvements.

TRANSITIONING TO PROCESS OWNER

The desired day has come. It's time to transition the monitoring and control to the process owner. Communication is vital during this period. You should have already been working closely with the process owner during the entire DMAIC process, so this transition should not come as a surprise to them.

Work closely with the team including the process owners to develop a transition plan, which might look like this:

Transitions to Who?	What?	When?	How?	Responsible Parties
Betty Clark – Director, Call Center Operations	Metric reporting and monitoring	3/1	Paul Tutor on Betty's team to report metrics weekly to Betty	Paul Tutor and Betty Clark

If it's a new process and there is no clear business owner, you will need to determine in the initial discussions who will own the process and assume regular oversight once the process is in place and stabilized. Otherwise, your team could get saddled with unnecessary ongoing oversight for one process which will inhibit your ability to pursue other process improvements as previously mentioned, or the established process could fall flat in just a few months as no one is overseeing it.

ROBOTIC PROCESS AUTOMATION (RPA)

RPA CENTER OF EXCELLENCE (COE) STEERING TEAM

SO, YOU HAVE DECIDED that automation will be helpful to your enterprise. Now what? It's essential to establish not only policies and procedures but also automation champions within your enterprise. Most likely, you will experience resistance — either from desk-level employees afraid that automations will take their jobs or management concerned that the bots might go crazy and take over the company. In the latter case, bots taking over the world or enterprise is the stuff of science fiction movies, not reality.

Even though the bots will not suddenly go crazy on their own and steal money from the enterprise, you will have to establish trust in your methodology for managing automations and monitoring and controlling their use. The bots won't go wild and become fraudulent but people sure can. The best way to establish trust in your automation program across your enterprise is to involve stakeholders in the establishment of the policies and procedures from the very beginning.

I strongly recommend that you start slow and establish a proven track record and adequate policies and procedures. Once these are well-established, you can scale quickly as you will have adequate guardrails in place.

Some of the stakeholders that should be included are:

- IT
- IT security
- IT server team (infrastructure)
- ID management
- Audit
- Risk management
- Reconciliation
- Operations
- SOX (compliance), if applicable

Start with a kickoff meeting. Be organized in how you present the opportunity. Make sure you don't come across as a salesperson but do try to state facts and metrics that demonstrate the benefit to the enterprise as a whole.

- What is the state of your enterprise now?
- Where do the stakeholders want it to be?

- How will that be achievable without automation?

Include time for everyone to express their concerns and document them. At the very beginning of the meeting, it's a good idea to tell the team you will be asking them all to provide input and concerns after you have given the overview.

Try to guide the steering team to address concerns not just express them. For example, ask those with concerns if they can research their concerns further and report back at the next steering team meeting with solutions to mitigate the concern if possible. If necessary, remind them where the enterprise might be in 2, 3, 4, 10 years against competition that are automated if your enterprise is not.

Establish a cadence of follow-up meetings. I generally have a meeting every 2 weeks for 30 minutes as it's not too demanding for those with heavy workflows, offers enough time to follow up on action items, and keeps the initiative alive and moving forward. If your enterprise is committed to a more progressive timeframe and have allotted the time for stakeholders to participate adequately so that the initiative can proceed more quickly, this is even better.

SOFTWARE

One of the biggest decisions for you and your steering team is which RPA software your enterprise will use. As soon as possible, start contacting potential vendors to determine what is needed to conduct Proof of Concepts (PoC's) with their software. If possible, lay this groundwork prior to your first kickoff meeting with your steering team.

As part of the kickoff, present the software options and preliminary pros and cons of each.

- Do you plan to select software that requires more coding experience or does your enterprise prefer software that is easier to learn to use?
- Do you want your program to fund itself as much as possible or will there be a large investment on the front end?

You may not know the answers to these questions, and they may be questions that your steering team needs to answer. Depending on the route you take, RPA software can run into six digits or more annually. The determination of the model of funding most likely will be driven from the executive level.

Once the software is selected, it's good to have a contract with your selected software vendor that allows for growth and additional license purchases for a set price during the terms of the contract. This way, you can grow and add licenses without going back to the negotiation table each time.

For example, our initial contract was for a 3-year period with the ability to purchase additional licenses during that period at the established price. Make sure you understand fully the type licenses you are purchasing.

LICENSES

License Types

a. Studio/Development

Typically, RPA software providers have licenses that are intended to be used by developers to develop the automations — not to run the automations on a regular basis once developed. There may also be an option for non-production studio/development licenses that others can use for troubleshooting and viewing the automation workflow without being able to create or change the automation.

As your CoE grows, these non-production licenses may become very useful. Be sure to check with the vendors whether they have this option.

Another factor to keep in mind is whether you intend for the automations to all be created by developers in the CoE or whether you would like to expand eventually to enable employees themselves to develop simpler automations.

When employees themselves create the automations, they are typically called Citizen Developers.

Most initiatives don't start out standing up a CoE and a Citizen Developer program at the same time. Negotiating with the software companies on the front end to purchase additional studio/development licenses at the established price during the contract period will allow the initiative to expand to Citizen Developers later without having to make the decision at the front end or go back into negotiations.

b. *Attended Robot*

The basic types of RPA licenses are attended and unattended. Attended automations are automations that are started and run by individual employees. The software is installed on individual machines and the employees open the software and start the automation when they desire.

There are multiple reasons why employees may want this option. The first is the reassurance of watching what the automation is doing. Your enterprise may prefer the first automations to be attended automations. Being able to watch the automations working and having control may be important for your employees. As the employees became more comfortable with the automations, you should be able to transition to unattended automations as confidence and comfort levels improve.

Some automations may also require employee approval or input. These are more suited for attended automations.

c. **Unattended Robot**

Unattended automations are automations that are scheduled and started by the software itself. This is typically managed through the software "control tower" or Orchestrator. The automations can typically be scheduled using either queue triggers, which start the automations when transactions are available in a queue or time triggers where the automations are scheduled to run at a certain time.

Licensing Model

Some questions to ask to determine the best licensing model are:

1. How often and how long the automations will run? How much of the day will they be needed? What time of the day will they be needed?

2. What is the impact if licenses are unavailable? Is this a time-critical process? Does it cause a customer-facing delay? What is the employee impact?

3. Is there a way to make a process improvement to address the process differently to provide the same level of customer and/or employee service or better but include some flexibility in license use timing?

4. How long will you be tied to this number of licenses? Can this be renegotiated?

Make sure you understand all the types of licenses the software providers offer. Don't just rely on the information the salesperson gives you. This is a large and very important investment and decision. Spend time researching the provider's licensing model and understanding their terminology. Time spent now will save you time in the future.

Once your CoE is operational, make use of the dashboards that are available within the RPA platform itself. You should be able to view license usage over time to determine whether you are bumping up against your capacity too closely. If your platform doesn't provide these type dashboards, consider building your own dashboards for license use monitoring using Tableau, Power BI, Elastic Kibana, or similar software. In the long run, these dashboards and analytics can save your enterprise a substantial amount of money.

ORCHESTRATOR MANAGEMENT

RPA software typically has a centralized control platform for managing licenses, starting unattended automations, accessing logs, creating variables and parameters, and housing commonly used activity packages. Some call this control tower the Orchestrator. Wherever you see the terminology "Orchestrator" in this book, it can be interpreted as the RPA's software "control tower".

Orchestrator Accesses

Most software providers' control tower/Orchestrators allow the creation of separate "tenants" to enable users to be separated and not have access to or view automations of other departments or teams if desired.

If you're in a highly regulated industry such as banking, Segregation of Duties (SOD) will be a factor when setting access permissions. In these industries, it's important that proper change management is in place and that developers are not allowed to migrate new automations to production. Work very closely with your steering team to decide on change management policies and procedures to help ensure SOD compliance.

After that, it's essential to incorporate these policies into the structure of your permissions to prevent issues. In the quality (continuous process improvement) world, this is called "poka-yoke". The Wikipedia definition of poka-yoke is: "any mechanism in a process that helps an equipment operator avoid (yokeru) mistakes (poka) defects by preventing, correcting, or drawing attention to human errors as they occur." Indeed, the best way to deal with errors is to prevent them in the first place.

There are typically default access roles provided in RPA software packages. You may find that these roles do not fit your needs. Consider creating your own specific roles according to your team's roles and responsibilities. The roles and accesses should be different in your QA and PROD environments to provide control. These are examples of possible roles:

Role Name	Description
Administrator	This is the highest level of access. It provides access for provisioning other accesses, adding machines, managing licenses, etc. More than one employee should have this access.
CoE lead	This role has all the access of the administrator but cannot create new roles for accesses to ensure Segregation of Duties (SOD) in a SOX enterprise. It is best to also not provision this role to employees who can create, edit, or store the automation code in the code repository.
Code migration agent	This role has access to migrate packages to production and create parameters and assets/variables. This is an elevated access and is not provisioned to developers or managers who manage developers to help ensure SOD. The code migration agent cannot have access to modify and save in code repository.
Business analyst (BA)	This role provides visibility to view jobs, queues, assets, etc.
Developer manager	This role provides visibility to view jobs, queues, assets, and so on in production. It does not have access to migrate. It can create and delete assets, parameters, queues, jobs, and so on in QA but not in production.
Developer	This role provides visibility to view jobs, queues, assets, and so on in production. It does not have access to migrate. It can create and delete assets, parameters, queues, jobs, and so on in QA but not in production.
Production monitoring	This role provides visibility to monitor jobs, level 1 troubleshooting, and rerun jobs.

The next step is to specify the access privileges aligned with each role for each environment. You will need a matrix for each environment. The easiest way to accomplish this is using Excel spreadsheets. Create a sheet for each environment: one sheet for Production, one for QA, etc. Then add columns to the right for each level of access.

Additional columns may include queues, triggers, processes, etc.

TEAM ROLE NAME	ASSETS			PACKAGES			ROBOTS		
	Create	Modify	Delete	Create	Modify	Delete	Create	Modify	Delete
Administrator									
CoE lead									
Code migration agent									
Business analyst (BA)									
Developer manager									
Developer									
Production monitoring									

Run Logs

Whatever RPA platform you select, there should be different levels of logging available that provide insight into what is happening when the automation is running. These choices range from the very basic information logging to verbose logging where there may be thousands of lines of logging during automation runs.

There are tradeoffs to be considered when selecting the level of logging desired. Typically, logging can be set at the user machine level, i.e., Susan's logging can be set different than Bot #3. Although verbose logging is very helpful to have, it also uses a lot of memory for storage. You may want to consider using verbose logging during hypercare periods or where automations have been problematic. Then, revert to information-only logging when the automation is stabilized. It's helpful to set a reminder on your calendar to revert to trace or lower-level logging, so you don't inadvertently have unnecessary verbose logging consuming your database.

In addition, log data may be stored in two different locations, where regular logging "clean up" should be conducted. The first is on local machines if your platform default is to store logs on local machines. Consider updating your configuration files to have log files stored on a central share drive or database where it will be easier to perform regular maintenance. Then proactively plan for regular maintenance. How long do you want to keep these files? You may also be able to limit the amount or number of logs stored locally by setting a parameter in your software platform's configuration file. Discuss with your provider and your team.

At first, you may want to keep logs for a more conservative length of time, then review in a few months to see whether the saved files needed to be accessed and revise your retention time accordingly.

Work with your IT department (or your technical expert if you work for a smaller operation) to determine what your log file maintenance will be. Do this proactively to avoid issues like the ones we encountered.

This sheet may be used for your planning:

LOG LOCATION	PLAN	INTERVAL	RESPONSIBLE PARTY (IES)
Example: unattended machines	Change default parameter in config file to limit local storage	Continuous	RPA CoE - John Smith
Example: database	Delete/archive files over 30 days old	Weekly (Automated script run)	Database team (point of contact = Don Brown)

INFRASTRUCTURE

SERVERS

If you plan to have unattended automations, you will need servers stood up for use. Even if you don't currently plan to use unattended automations, there is a very high likelihood that you will in the future. During the time spent with your steering team, make sure that IT has read and understood fully the requirements for servers and agrees that the servers can be stood up for unattended automations and the timeframe required to accomplish this. Purchasing unattended licenses prior to IT's ability to stand up the servers needed is wasteful.

ACCESS PROVISIONING AND STORAGE

ACCESSES

To work properly, automations and developers must be provisioned access to the platforms, systems, and shared drives needed for the automation. Access provisioning can be one of the most time-consuming tasks blocking the beginning of development for automations. There are basically three types of accesses you will need to concentrate on and have policies and procedures to manage.

i. The first are active directory accesses that the unattended bots need to have basic single sign-on accesses like employees. Single sign-on means that usernames and passwords are not required.

ii. The second type are accesses needed for mainframe applications.

iii. The third type of accesses are non-mainframe access such as web applications.

Both the second and third type require usernames and passwords.

Work closely with the ID management team or the team tasked with access provisioning and the rest of the steering team to determine the best way for provisioning access for your automations. You may decide to use contractor ID's, service accounts or other means for this purpose. Also work with the steering team to determine the naming convention for automation accesses. Naming conventions are helpful as they provide a means for your team as well as others in the enterprise when a process has been completed by an automation rather than an employee. This quick identification enables others to know who to contact if needed.

It is helpful to also have some reference to the automation or automations the accesses provisioned are running. This will help your team in the future as the number of automations you have running in production grows.

For non-mainframe/web or other accesses, work closely with the application owner to determine what is required for usernames and passwords.

CREDENTIAL SECURITY

To ensure proper credential storage and rotation, work closely with your IT security team. Most RPA software platforms have integration with credential storage platforms such as CyberArk. Take advantage of these applications as soon as possible to utilize their automated password rotation capabilities as well as secure storage and structured password checkout features.

You will also need to decide who will have access to checkout passwords. If you are in a highly regulated environment, take into consideration Segregation of Duties (SOD) requirements. It may be advisable depending on your enterprise and industry to not allow anyone with the ability to update and modify automations to have access to check out production passwords. Additional considerations to restrict access to check out production passwords should be considered.

Your team may need to check out passwords for troubleshooting purposes. This allows logging onto machines and/or mainframe platforms to visually observe them and better understand what may be causing failures. Take into consideration whether it is advisable for those that can change code to also have the ability to access production passwords. You may want to have intermediaries on your team obtain the production passwords and share screen with developers.

Also, any passwords required for updating licensing or upgrading software even if not performed by CoE employees should be stored in a centralized, secure password repository such as CyberArk. If someone leaves your enterprise and has not put passwords in a centralized repository, you may spend wasted time to gain back accesses. This can be avoided by storing passwords in a password repository.

ROLES AND RESPONSIBILITIES

Document and clearly define the roles and responsibilities of each team member. This is an example of the possible roles and responsibilities:

TEAM ROLE NAME	ROLES AND RESPONSIBILITIES
Director — RPA and process improvement	Strategic guidance, control compliance, policies and procedures' creation and development, program marketing and growth, opportunity identification, prioritization, continuous internal efficiency improvements, and ROI achievement. This role may not exist in the beginning depending on the size of your initiative and role may be combined with the RPA CoE lead.
RPA CoE lead	Day-to-day management of throughput, policies, and procedures and adherence, monitoring, troubleshooting, access provisioning.
BA manager	Manages throughput and quality of PDDs and oversees meetings with business process owners for PDD approvals and automation demos.
BA	Works with business process owners to create and enhance PDDs and works with business process owners as the "bridge" between developers and the business process owners for enhancements and clarifications.
Developer manager	Manages and ensures throughput quality, responsible for change management adherence, and code reviews. Manages hypercare, monitors automations during hypercare, and assists with production troubleshooting and management. Does not have the ability to migrate packages to retain SOD.
Developer	Develops automations in adherence to PDD requirements, conducts and documents User Acceptance Testing (UAT), works with process owners and BAs during hypercare, and monitors automations during hypercare. Does not have the ability to migrate packages to retain SOD.
Production monitoring	Monitors jobs, level 1 troubleshooting (can expand to higher levels of troubleshooting as CoE grows), and reruns jobs.
Migration agent	Highly restricted. No one with ability to modify automations can migrate to production to ensure SOD.

TEAM MODEL

BUILDING YOUR TEAM

One of the challenges you will face is hiring the right people and putting them in the right position. Even with the best of intent and interviewing and vetting process, some of your hires may not work out as hoped. Others will but will leave for better opportunities. Be methodical and clear about your expectations for everyone. The more visibility tracking metrics can be provided by way of dashboards and scrum trackers, the better.

If done properly, your entire team will be continuously aware of the pipeline. Even though you will aim for everyone on the team to take ownership and be proactive in making sure they're contributing to the team's success to the highest extent, there will be some who inevitably have all the apparent traits of a successful team member but don't live up to expectations.

This doesn't just happen in RPA programs, as you know. However, the fast-moving nature of an RPA program requires vigilance and difficult decisions to provide maximum benefit to the enterprise. Make sure you keep growing and going. Don't allow those who don't take ownership and do their share to drag down your program(s).

These people will either come onboard and decide to be positive, productive, and take ownership or they will remain negative, in which case you will need to deal with them. You *really* need A players across the board to do the best job you can for your enterprise. Don't let bad apples spoil everything for everybody.

Keep focused on your responsibility. You have been hired to do this job and to do the best you can for the enterprise. Individuals cannot be allowed to destroy that potential for the enterprise. Deal with it and move on. Focus on the positive and the positive individuals. Do not think it is unique to the enterprise where you are now. You will deal with this in any enterprise — even those where the grass looks greener. The grass is not greener. The challenges will just come with different faces and different names, but they will be there.

Other challenges in getting the right people in the right place may come from circumstances beyond your control such as mergers or acquisitions. As your program grows or unexpected changes due to mergers or acquisitions happen, you will need to adapt your model determining new needs and their respective go to models. Don't let this take you by surprise – embrace it.

In addition, automations in production will need to be enhanced to adapt to system upgrades, software upgrades, and so on. Remember that with RPA and process improvement — **nothing** stays the same. Practice what you preach and not only embrace but look forward to change.

INHOUSE VS. CONTRACTED

At some point, you will most likely face decisions whether to contract resources or hire them. Multiple factors go into the best decision for your enterprise. Do you expect the volume of work you have to remain constant? Do you live in a location where qualified employees are readily available or are you open to remote employees? Currently, the volume of work staying the same and having qualified employees readily available in specific locations is relatively rare.

If this is the case, you may want to consider contracting at least part of your workforce. That way someone else manages turnover and replacements and you can concentrate on growing your program. You may also want to balance employees versus contract employees to provide a stable base and continuity with the ability to expand or contract easily.

When making the decision about standing up your monitoring team, you may want to consider the advantages and disadvantages of going with a contract model versus hiring internally. The advantages of contracting include that the contracting company manages hiring, training, backfill and vacation coverage. If hired as an employee, additional staff would have to be trained and available to monitor during vacations, illness, etc. You also are at risk if the employee gives notice as you must spend time interviewing, hiring, and training, and another employee's time would be diverted to monitoring rather than creating new automations during the transition period. Disadvantages to contracting out roles includes lessened control over hiring and in some cases higher turnover.

PROCESS

POLICIES AND PROCEDURES

When you first stand up your RPA CoE, there will be no established policies and procedures. You must start somewhere. Open a new Word document and title it "RPA CoE Policies and Procedures Draft" and get started. As you continue to establish your policies and procedures, add them to your document.

It will be helpful to establish a Table of Contents (ToC) from the start. I base my ToC on outline levels in Word. This enables easy updating of the ToC as the document grows. Search for "table of contents outline levels on the internet if you're not familiar with how to do this. You will need to occasionally view your outline formatting and clean up if you use this type of table of contents, but I have found this type TOC a very good way to achieve a well-organized TOC. It also provides the advantage of being able to navigate quickly to sections using the navigation panel in Word.

Links for resources can be found at
www.theleanmission.com.

ASSESS AND PRIORITIZE

After you've identified opportunities, you will need to do a preliminary assessment diving a bit deeper. These assessments can range from a few basic questions to more in-depth spreadsheets that help you determine the amount of effort required for development.

As a start, you should obtain the answers to the following questions if you didn't when the opportunity was first identified:

- Volume (transactions/year):
- Time/transaction:
- Potential time savings/year (volume * time/transaction):
- Is there volume growth expected in the future that will encumber the existing team and manual processing if not automated?
- Systems/platforms involved:
- Are there anticipated changes to the involved systems/platforms? If so, how soon?
- Do the process owners currently have time to spend with the RPA team? What are their time restrictions, if any?
- Is the input standardized or does it come in free form?
- Can any "human" judgement aspects be expressed in clear statements such as "If this happens, then do this, else do that"?

Whether you will automate if system changes are anticipated will be a decision that management will need to make based upon the needs of the enterprise. If your enterprise is involved in a merger or acquisition with anticipated volume growth while experiencing attrition, it may be desirable to automate processes that you wouldn't otherwise to provide the short-term lift needed.

Beware of projected timeframes provided to you if other resources are needed to achieve process improvements. It isn't a lie when someone tells you it will take 2 months and it ends up not being completed a year down the road — other teams also have bandwidth restrictions. They may intend to have it completed in 2 months but have other tasks that are prioritized for them to accomplish.

If you're new to your company, ask someone who has been there for a while: "Does this group tend to be able to predict accurately how long something takes or does it tend to take longer than anticipated?"

I remember vividly a meeting in the conference room in one of my positions when I reported that we were improving a process and would be moving to a digital form solution. IT had told me the solution would be complete and available in a month. The execs in the room just laughed and laughed. I asked why they were laughing, and they basically said there is no way IT would have it done in a month.

I left that meeting and thought they were *so* jaded and cynical. IT said they would have it done in a month, and I trusted they would. A year later, not only did IT not have that form solution completed but they had not even developed a plan and identified a platform for creating digital forms. I don't want to say I became jaded and cynical after that — I would prefer to say I became more realistic. It is best to get to know the reality of capabilities of providing solutions rather than wished for goals.

Additional factors may play havoc with anticipated schedules such as unexpected production issues, competing priorities, and illness. Once the information is obtained from the assessments, you will need to prioritize. Prioritization decisions need to be made by the RPA director, if there is one, or the RPA CoE lead if there is no RPA director. Some enterprises may prefer these decisions to be made by a steering team or upper-level management.

Keep in mind that if a steering team is making the prioritization decisions, the RPA team may not be able to produce at full capacity. Why? Because delays waiting for decisions from the steering team may cause unused down time for resources. I have found that being able to be agile and prioritize according to resources' bandwidth (which can change rapidly) and our stakeholders' needs enables resources to be utilized more flexibly and efficiently, minimizing downtime.

Prioritizations should be based on the strategic goals and priorities. These may change rapidly depending on growth and demand, so prepare to be nimble in your prioritization.

If you are working through a merger or acquisition, your priorities may be to continue to provide customer improvements and create merger-related automations and automations that help employees deliver quality transaction achievement during a period of high growth.

It's vital to understand the **importance of proactive capacity creation**. For areas anticipating high volume growth, automating in these areas can ensure continued high levels of operational quality, reduce employee stress, and improve customer service during these periods of growth.

Bots don't need to sleep, cook dinner, pick up children, pay attention to family members and/or spouses, etc. Let the bots take the heavy lift off employees and avoid employee burnout and turnover. It's best to save employees' time and energy for the items that require human decision-making, touch, or interaction.

If your employees are overtaxed, they are highly unlikely to be nice and friendly over time. Don't continue to overtax them and expect that they will provide the level of customer service needed to retain and grow your customer base.

PROCESS DEFINITION DOCUMENT (PDD)

PDD Creation

If you work on-site with the process owners, you may be able to communicate with them easily as you have questions. You may be able to walk over to their desks and ask them questions and get clarification.

However, as your team grows and particularly if you add offshore resources, your PDDs will need to become more detailed. Offshore developers will need keystroke by keystroke descriptions, screenshots, explanations, etc. There are several ways to accomplish obtaining the screenshots. The very basic way is to take pictures with your phone. This will be time consuming though as you must ask the operator to pause for you to capture.

The better way is to record the employees as they perform the process on a call and use the screenshots from the recording for your documentation. There is also software on the market that can be loaded on the employee's computer that captures the screenshots and keystrokes and creates an initial PDD. If you consider using this type software, be sure to test the software and make sure passwords are not captured.

It's very important to do your own due diligence when assessing software of this type. Don't just believe what the software companies are telling you. Test it and review it.

Prior to starting the actual work on a PDD, you will need to create a PDD template that will be used for your documentation. Most of the RPA software vendors can provide a template or you can obtain one on the internet and adapt it to your specific needs.

The first step in starting your PDD documentation is to schedule a kickoff call with the process owner. The BA and/or BA manager should schedule this call. I like to schedule 30 minutes.

It helps greatly if you record these calls as previously discussed as the BA will be able to obtain screenshots for the PDD from the recording. The employee most familiar with the process will need to share their screen during the call and walk through the steps in the process. Even if you are in person, it may help to have a "call" to enable the ability to record. But be sure to verify with everyone on the call that it's acceptable to record.

Additional calls will be required for clarifications.

PDD Reviews

When your initial PDD is completed, schedule a meeting/call to review the PDD with the business process owners, i.e., subject matter experts (SMEs). It's surprising how much additional information comes out during these reviews.

If new information surfaces, update the PDD and schedule another meeting/call to review the update. Continue this process until no new information comes forth. It's far easier to make these discoveries at this stage in the process. In the long run, time spent making sure as much as possible is included in the PDD will pay off.

Unfortunately, even with the greatest diligence during PDD creation, there will still be surprises that surface during development and when the automation is migrated to production. Don't be too judgmental about the BA or SMEs. It's difficult to accurately nail down all the scenarios that can occur. Although we aim to improve this continuously, additions and edits to the first drafts of the PDD will still occur.

When the business process owners, BA, and BA Manager believe the PDD is ready to move to development, the business process owner needs to do a final review of the PDD, and the BA needs to obtain an "official" approval of the PDD indicating that it's ready to move to development.

DEVELOPMENT

PDD Handoff

Development begins with a meeting between the BA and developer to review the PDD. The BA schedules this meeting and reviews the PDD with the developer. If the developer has questions that the BA can't answer, the BA goes back to the business process owner for clarification.

Solution Design Document (SDD)

The developer then reviews the automation flow and creates the SDD. In the SDD, it's best for the developer to include how they intend the automation to flow based on the PDD. They should also include the list of variables.

It is beneficial to schedule regular design review calls with the developers to review the SDDs prior to development. All developers should attend these calls to not only learn but also provide input. Efficiency and quality are improved due to these reviews as developers share insights and best practices. In some cases, parts of the automation have already been built for other automations and can be utilized. These calls provide a platform and time for this knowledge to be exchanged.

Time spent for these reviews not only provides a better product but also enables us to avoid time-consuming code changes. Keep in mind that depending on the change management required by your enterprise, even small changes may require change orders, approvals, etc.

SDD templates are available on the internet. Links for resources can be found at www.theleanmission.com.

Development and Best Practices

Variables should not be hard coded into the automations but stored as either assets or in a config file so they can be easily edited if needed. The following is a partial list of items that are better stored outside the automation code itself. Storing these items outside the code will help the CoE respond more nimbly to changes.

- Email addresses
- Email subject lines
- Email bodies (store in .txt file)
- File and folder paths
- Delay times

When the developer has completed the automation, the BA schedules a demo with the business process owner(s). If the business process owner has changes, the BA updates the PDD, and the developer incorporates the changes into the automation.

After completing the changes, the BA schedules another demo until the business process owners are satisfied with the automation and give their approval to proceed to production. Once the business process owners have approved the automations, a code review is conducted either by another developer or manager, then the developer completes the User Acceptance Testing (UAT) documentation.

You may use a simple Excel spreadsheet for your UAT showing basic facts and some high-level steps like the following:

Automation Name:			Conducted By:	
UAT Date:			Pass/Fail:	

STEP	Description	Expected Outcome	Pass/Fail	Comment	Screenshot

The code review should be standardized to make sure all developers are adhering to the same guidelines. During the code review, items such as hard-coded variables should be checked. Also, the automation should be developed so that others can easily follow the flow to facilitate monitoring and troubleshooting.

It's helpful to create a second tab in the code review spreadsheet listing the elements included in the code review. This is a living document and can/should be continuously improved.

Automation Code Storage

It's best practice not to have automation code stored on individual computers. If an employee becomes ill or is unexpectedly off, it's essential that the code be readily available for others to maintain business continuity. This is also important if employees leave their positions, and particularly if they leave the company.

We mitigate this risk in two ways. The first is that our automation code and associated documentation are stored on a shared drive according to the folder structure discussed in the next section. The second factor is that our developers are required to store their code in our code storage platform. The code can then be checked out for view only or for modification.

MIGRATION TO PRODUCTION

After the UAT and code review are completed, it's time to migrate to production. Depending on the controls in place, you may need to create a change order and go through an approval process. You also may be restricted at certain times from migration to production if your enterprise views automations in the same light as system changes. Many enterprises have black out periods when migrations of new "code" cannot take place. The original intent for these blackout periods is to help ensure system stability during critical periods.

If your enterprise views automations the same as system changes, your automations will not be able to migrate during system change freeze periods. Make sure you know ahead of time what the migration policy will be. Work closely with the IT department that controls change to ensure you're compliant and agree on the change policy for your automations.

Prior to migrating, make sure the values of the variables in your automation have been documented and updated to reflect their value in production. These will be different between the development and production environments. Also, make sure the proper accesses have been provisioned.

For unattended automations, it is important to log on to your production machines and manually check that accesses have been provisioned properly.

Migration Plans and Methods

Consider rolling out the automations you have that are going to large volumes of users in a phased approach. Perhaps start with 10% of users. Monitor license usage. Add licenses if needed. Add another 20%. Again, monitor license usage and add if needed. Continue this phased rollout until the entire population is in production.

You can roll these out in 1–2 week increments or other increments. Some time spent with this phased roll-out can save time in the long run.

For large rollouts, I recommend an implementation plan that puts a new automation into production every 2 weeks with a phased-in number of users to provide time for license monitoring and additional license purchases, as follows:

LEAN MISSION

Automation	Week 1	Week 3	Week 5	Week 7	Week 9	Week 11	Week 13	Week 15	Week 17
1	10% of users	+20% (30%)	+20% (50%)	+20% (70%)	+30% (100%)				
2		10% of users	+20% (30%)	+20% (50%)	+20% (70%)	+30% (100%)			
3			10% of users	+20% (30%)	+20% (50%)	+20% (70%)	+30% (100%)		
4				10% of users	+20% (30%)	+20% (50%)	+20% (70%)	+30% (100%)	
5					10% of users	+20% (30%)	+20% (50%)	+20% (70%)	+30% (100%)

Depending on your enterprise and timing needs, you can expedite these phases to have a quicker rollout. You can also compress the rollout as you add the automations. You will have increasingly more data regarding license use as you continue to add users and analyze license usage. This data and analysis will be increasingly helpful, particularly if the automations and usage are similar.

You may wonder why this type of rollout might be necessary as you should be able to predict many elements of the rollout during design. However, items/issues occur occasionally that were not predicted. In many cases, you are dealing with front-end users who do not always know, interpret, and initiate as requested.

You may need to adjust error messages and handling. You also may experience higher or lower volumes than predicted, which will impact the number of licenses required.

Of course, if you have a time-critical, urgent need, the phased approach is not advisable or practical.

HYPERCARE

In your schedule, you should also incorporate a period of hypercare when the automation is monitored closely to help ensure the automation is performing stably and as intended. Typically, this is a three-week period. During this period, developers and BAs should be prepared to respond quickly if needed to update PDDs and automations and changes required in production.

Be careful when planning BA and developer time and loads to incorporate ample time for these hypercare periods. Also, if you are subject to migration freezes, do not migrate new automations just prior to a freeze as it may be difficult to be responsive with changes needed to address production challenges.

Be very clear who is monitoring during the hypercare period and what is expected of them. Typically, the developer should monitor during this period. Make sure the developer clearly understands this. They should continue to monitor until the automation has proven that it is performing as expected *and* the monitoring has been turned over to someone else if it's an unattended automation.

It may be helpful to include a requirement for developers to provide a regular report on the automation. This reporting will ensure that monitoring is taking place as required.

MAINTENANCE

Incident Management and Reporting

As part of any automation program, issues will inevitably occur. Plan for this. Determine how you want the incidents to be reported, how the issues will be addressed and resolved and how communication will be provided. It will be helpful to you to be proactive in creating a form and workflow for reporting issues. The workflow should include regular communication with impacted parties to notify them of the employee assigned to address the issue and progress toward addressing and resolution.

Monitoring

As your program grows, your team will spend increasingly more time monitoring automations in production. This will take away from the time your team is able to spend developing new automations. For many enterprises, a critical decision point when considering different options for handling monitoring, production troubleshooting, and maintenance occurs when you have between 40 and 50 automations in production. Of course, this is dependent on the size of your team though and whether your team has expanded as the number of automations increased to provide extra bandwidth for monitoring and troubleshooting.

As you grow, stay aware of how the production maintenance side of your program is impacting the bandwidth available for new developments and growth. There will be management decisions that need to be made. Does management want the program to continue to grow — or are they satisfied with just staying at a certain number of automations and size? Unfortunately, they cannot have their cake and eat it too. There are limits in bandwidth availability that will be reached.

While you should be continuously making efforts to improve the efficiency of your own RPA and process improvement programs, there will still be bandwidth limits. Have frank proactive discussions with management about this.

Production Troubleshooting

There are several levels of production troubleshooting. Level 1 troubleshooting is when more basic machine/automation restarts are required due to connection or access loss, etc. There may also be times when an unexpected screen pops up during execution, causing the automation to fault. Level 1 troubleshooting can log onto the machine, clear the unexpected screen, and restart the automation. However, they should also report this occurrence to management so the developers can enhance the automation to handle the screen or other issues if possible.

The automation may also fault due to unexpected and intermittent latency, where the Level 1 troubleshooting can restart the automation to determine if the latency is intermittent. This also needs to be reported to management as delays may need to be introduced in the automation or increased to prevent future issues.

If initial attempts using Level 1 troubleshooting are not successful, the monitoring team will need to escalate this. Determine what the escalation policy will be. Who will the issue be reported to initially? What is the process once reported?

Your developer manager may be the next step as they should be knowledgeable in how the automations work and may be able to provide the next level of troubleshooting. If they're unable to identify and rectify the issue, a developer will need to be engaged.

Keep in mind that as the number of automations in production grows, so will the time that developers need for troubleshooting. Their production of new automations cannot continue at the same pace as initial production. Determine how much time a developer needs to help with troubleshooting and be cognizant of this time when assigning new automations.

BUSINESS CONTINUITY – BACKUP PLANS AND COMMUNICATION

Assuming automations and the underlying systems they depend on will always work as intended is foolhardy. Issues happen. Systems go out. Plan for it before you put your first automation into production.

Have and document a backup plan for cases where the automation doesn't work as intended. Typically, the backup plan will be that the process will have to be performed manually by the business unit instead. In your PDDs, include a section called "Detailed Process," detailing the step-by-step process the developer would need for the automation to perform.

When you go to production, provide the documentation to the business process owners. They will be able to use the detailed steps section as the start of a Job Aid that they should maintain in the case manual processing is required. It is important for them to maintain any changes to the job aid themselves in case manual processing is needed. As they become more dependent upon the automation and attrition occurs, the knowledge pertaining to manual processing will be lost and an up-to-date job aid will be essential. If you have a business continuity department, it will be beneficial to include them in establishing the policies and procedures for business continuity. It is not advisable that your automation department become responsible for the maintenance of the manual job aids as it would take your resources away from automation production and monitoring which should be your core focus.

CONTROL AND MANAGEMENT

Standardization

As your RPA program grows, so will the variability in your deliverables — unless you have processes in place that ensure consistency. If processes aren't in place to standardize, you will find that as soon as you plug one leaky hole in your boat, another one will spring forth.

It is important to recognize that by nature, processes that are not controlled will tend toward chaos or entropy. The definition of entropy provided by Wikipedia at https://en.wikipedia.org/wiki/Entropy is, "Entropy is a scientific concept as well as a measurable physical property that is most commonly associated with a state of disorder, randomness, or uncertainty."

So, what to do? How do we counteract this natural tendency to disorder? Focus on putting processes in place that will help ensure consistency, adherence to best practice standards, and accountability. In doing so, you will also improve the communication of expectations to your team and reinforce expectations.

Focus on PnP. What is PnP? **Processes not people**. It's very important to focus on putting processes in place to ensure consistency. If these processes aren't in place, your program will experience so much variability that you will be so involved in plugging holes and trying to standardize that you won't be able to focus on improvements.

What processes do you need to ensure standardization, adherence, and accountability? Process flowcharts with roles and responsibilities for each step and the members of your team are helpful. Some of the phases to include in this flowchart along with the roles/responsibilities and ownership for each are provided here:

- Initial opportunity identification
- Assess
- PDD
- Development
- Migration/change management
- Hypercare
- Production monitoring

What else do you need to put into place?

- Checklists for each of these categories, itemizing the processes and roles and responsibilities for each step
- Monitoring and follow-up plans
    - ◊ Who will review to report adherence and "slippage" from standards?
    - ◊ How will these be handled and communicated?

Let's start with the checklists needed for each area:

- Initial opportunity identification

    ◊ Checklist

        ➤ Volume of transactions? (Is there anticipated volume increase expected?)

        ➤ Time/transaction provided?

        ➤ Systems involved?

        ➤ Anticipated system/process changes identified?

        ➤ Primary point of contact

- Assess

    ◊ Checklist

        ➤ High-level overview of the process steps

        ➤ Anticipated availability of SMEs and any blockers or scheduling challenges anticipated (These factors come into play and impact the time needed to complete the PDD as the BAs must often wait long periods for clarification, test data, etc.)

- PDD

    ◊ Checklist

        ➤ Flowcharts – current/proposed

- Detailed steps of process identified
- Exceptions and exception handling identified
- Audit logging – template and paths (It is helpful to provide two copies of these logs: one that the business can access to address exceptions and make comments and one not accessible by the business to be used by the CoE or audit department if needed)
- Accesses required
- Test data required and resource to obtain

- Development

  - Checklist

    - Solution Design Document (SDD) created and reviewed (This document details the approach the developer will take to automate the process; it's helpful to have and review to ensure everyone agrees to the planned approach prior to development)
    - Targeted completion date (Anticipated completion dates may often be missed due to delays waiting for test data, system outages etc., so add an additional column titled "Targeted Completion Date (Updated)". This will help you track what the original anticipated completion date was and how it had to be revised. Having this level of

information, may help improve your future estimations.

➤ Demo to business owners

* The BA schedules the demo with the process owners. This provides an additional check to help ensure that no components have been left out. The process owners must approve the automation prior to finalization and migration to production.

➤ Code reviews are performed after process owner approval and prior to migration and are either conducted by another developer or the developer manager. As previously discussed, add another sheet to your User Acceptance Testing (UAT) that contains items to be checked during code review such as the items below:

* Activities appended with description to assist with easier navigation and troubleshooting

* No emails, paths, or other variables hard coded

* Library (reusable) modules used whenever possible

* Exceptions properly identified and handled

- > UAT completed
- Migration/Change Management
  - ◊ Checklist
    - > UAT provided
    - > Code review checked
    - > Change order (or your change management procedure followed)
    - > Automation placed in hypercare and clearly defined who will monitor
- Hypercare
  - ◊ Checklist
    - > Communication has been made with business unit regarding how the automation will be run during hypercare and oversight
    - > Developers/BAs understand the monitoring requirements, troubleshooting, enhancement, and change process

Now that you have the processes, standardization, and checklists in place, here comes the more difficult part. Ensuring adherence to standards and procedural processes can be very much like herding cats. This is the case particularly if you have team members who have previously been allowed to do everything their own way and are now having to make changes.

No matter how you word it, they may still want to do everything their own way. At some point, you may have to make the difficult decision to draw the line in the sand and say, "This is how it will be done." They will then have to make the decision for themselves whether they can live with the changes or improvements.

Indeed, try to use the word "improvement" rather than "change" when referring to the new processes and procedures. It's a small difference but a more positive spin. Either way, there will be those who don't like it. There may be turnover. Expect it, anticipate it, and plan for it. Don't let it take you by surprise. Have contingency plans in place for each person/position on your team and be diligent to help ensure that turnover impacts on your team are minimal and that your program is very agile.

While being aware of the importance of not micromanaging, be sure to also stay focused on standardization. This can be difficult to address but absolutely must be addressed as lack of standardization and regular reviews can lead to an increasing inability to stabilize these programs and have them grow and be sustainable.

Lack of standardization causes decreased efficiency and diminishes the positive factors that can be achieved by capitalizing on economies of scale. Think of lack of standardization as being like the wild, wild west with everyone running around energetically in many different directions with no focus and consistency and/or absence of goals and plans to attain goals.

You should anticipate that your team may resist standardization and view it as micromanagement. Make sure it's not micromanagement but is indeed standardization. Give them freedom within the policies and procedures to do their daily work as they see fit if they stay within the policies and procedures. Make sure you don't cross the line and start micromanaging.

According to Merriam-Webster, the definition of micromanagement is "to manage especially with excessive control or attention to details." You might find it helpful to read the Harvard Business Review article *Signs That You're a Micromanager* by Muriel Maignan Wilkins. (https://hbr.org/2014/11/signs-that-youre-a-micromanager)

Folder Structure

At the beginning of your program, you should standardize your folder structure. Starting with a standardized folder structure will save you spending time organizing it to a standard later.

A basic folder structure is as follows:

- 📁 AUTOMATION NAME
  - 📁 REQUIREMENTS
    - 📁 PDD
    - 📁 PROCESS MAPS
  - 📁 SOLUTION DESIGN
  - 📁 BUILD
    - 📁 CODE
    - 📁 TEST DATA
    - 📁 CONFIG FILES (DEVELOPMENT)
    - 📁 LOGS
  - 📁 DEPLOYMENT
    - 📁 RUNBOOKS
    - 📁 CONFIG FILES (PRODUCTION)
  - 📁 OTHERS (MISCELLANEOUS FILES)
    - 📁 UAT
  - 📁 CHANGE ORDERS
  - 📁 PACKAGES

It is also a time saver and efficiency gain to store the templates you need at different points in the process in the folders. Store the PDD and process map templates in the Requirements folder, the UAT template in the UAT folder etc..

Program Reviews

As your program(s) grow, whether continuous process improvement or RPA, you will most likely have to be retrospective occasionally and look at your programs' policies and procedures as well as the actual day-to-day processes and workings of your team(s). As you build these programs, particularly if they grow exponentially very quickly, there may be a time when you recognize that there is a lack of adequate policies and procedures or a lack of adherence to policies and procedures.

If you are in a larger enterprise, you may also come across others whose efforts at standardization will cause challenges in your efforts to ensure the growth of your RPA and process improvement initiatives.

I have experienced this multiple times with initiatives. What is needed to do to standardize and produce most efficiently contradicted some of the efforts other departments had taken to standardize their own systems, platforms, and processes. You may run up against the same challenges.

Go into these conversations seeking to understand and work collaboratively to reach the best win-win solution for all. What are they trying to achieve? Is there a way that your initiative can be successful and theirs as well? Be willing to be open-minded.

If you can function with some adaptations within their initiative needs, try to do so and be a good team player. If they cross the line and are no longer looking out for the best of the enterprise but wanting to dictate how you run your initiatives (regardless of the negative impact on the enterprise), be respectful and gently point this out to them. They are experts in their field and your team are experts in the fields of RPA and process improvement. If they can provide the options that are available to your team, your team has the expertise to decide which of the options will work best for your team's requirements.

If they continue to be controlling rather than enabling, it may be necessary to escalate. Do everything possible to come to a win-win prior to escalating. Upper-level management has a lot on its plate. If a solution can be agreed upon without their involvement, it's much preferred. While trying to ensure that your initiatives are successful, it's very important to keep the success of the entire enterprise as most important. At times, it may be necessary to remind others gently and respectfully of the importance of doing what is best for the enterprise as a whole.

Be careful not to assume you can tell others how to run their area of expertise, and make sure they are respectful of you and your team being experts in yours. These can be tricky conversations.

Ask more questions of them and sincerely try to understand their challenges as well as their goals. Hopefully, they will respond likewise and seek to understand your challenges and goals. This is a much more productive model for finding win-win solutions and achieving support from other departments.

If you're the one responsible for an initiative, make sure you identify all stakeholders and include them all as soon as possible. Not just the ones who agree with your opinions or direction but most importantly those who have an opposing view.

Listen to them. Is there a way to address their concerns by altering your path a bit? Don't just set your path and head straight forward with blinders on, not considering other departments' goals and requirements. You could very well get blindsided. It's essential to the success of your program to work collaboratively with other departments.

GAP Analysis

Performing a gap analysis at regular intervals can be beneficial toward continuously improving your RPA program.

- Where are you?
- Where do you want to be?
- What is the gap, i.e., what do you need to do to get from where you are to where you want to be?

Here, you will find the outcome of possible areas that may be identified in a gap analysis of an RPA program:

- Metric compilation extremely inefficient
    - Initial input in two different places with copy and paste required to keep synchronized
    - Inefficient status double entry tracking, i.e., tracking in master list but also have updates in other places
    - ROI spreadsheet separate from master list where automations are tracked
        - Need to link initial volume obtained during assessment to ROI
    - Need to add volume and time/transaction to PDD/assessment checklist
    - Systems not identified accurately
    - Volume and time per transaction not obtained or entered on the master list
    - Too much missing information
        - Need to complete historical metrics
            * Dates PDD completed
            * Dates Development completed
            * Dates migration to PROD completed
- Need to decrease repeated migration, particularly emergency migrations

- ◊ Track change orders/migrations per developer and reasons
- Automations are not standardized sufficiently
  - ◊ Need to improve UAT and code review checklist
  - ◊ Put into place processes and checks and balances to help ensure standard policies and procedure adherence
  - ◊ Use more library modules
- Share drive accesses are not tight, i.e., all accesses have read ability to all folders on the share drive
  - ◊ Perform regular access reviews
  - ◊ Create tighter controls for access
- Need for design reporting, monitoring, and oversight
  - ◊ Schedule meetings with team to determine KPIs and design dashboards

As you begin to work through gap analysis for your programs, the many facets of the programs that seem convoluted and not well put-together or connected may start to become clearer to you enabling you to make plans to close the gaps. It is beneficial to both track metrics in real time and regularly review updates to help ensure the integrity of the data is maintained. It is beneficial to schedule time specific for the purpose of discussing and reviewing improvement initiatives for your CoE and progress toward achieving goal completion. A good way to achieve this oversight is to schedule monthly meetings with your managers.

I prefer a format like the following to track gaps identified, develop a plan to close the gaps, and track completion:

GAP	PLAN	RESPONSIBLE PARTY	TARGET DATE	MILESTONE CHECKPOINTS
Synchronized automated updates	Review and develop plan for consolidating/synchronizing opportunity identification portal, RPA tracker and metric reporting	Laura	Plan due – July	Monthly – during team strategic planning meetings – put on monthly strategic planning agenda
Complete historical metrics	Obtain volumes and time per transaction for existing automations	Laura	Friday, 4/16	Every day
Libraries not utilized as much as possible	Review and determine what additional automated steps can be included as a reusable library	Developer manager	May	
Share drive accesses	Determine best way to restrict accesses	Technology manager	May	
Metric capture	Are metrics being consistently updated in master list?	Laura/managers	May	

Reporting

Reporting and how you design your dashboards and Key Performance Indicators (KPIs) will not only be important in running your program successfully but also in gaining support and helping ensure your program's benefit is accurately proven and shown in a transparent and accurate manner.

This can be challenging because when you start asking for volumes and time per transaction, many of the processes you will be automating will be manual processes. You will possibly be requesting funding for large expenditures, and you need to be able to prove that your metrics are dependable.

In some cases, the best you can get for volumes and time per transaction will be guesstimates. As your program matures, keep in mind that you will need a more objective, black, and white way to show volumes such as actual volume processed.

There are several ways to accomplish this tracking as your program matures. One way is to design your automations using queues for each trigger. This way, you will be able to track the actual number of transactions processed. The dispatcher/performer model can be used for this, which is a generic reusable automation that obtains transactions to be processed and puts them in the appropriate queue. The performer then picks them up and processes them.

You can also include a metric tracking module in your automations that will log the number of transactions processed by the automation each time it runs. This is helpful as it is important to accurately define what a transaction is and make sure it is in alignment with the metric provided for time for each transaction if processed manually. This becomes clearer as you are working on your return on investment (ROI) metrics. For example, an automation may process invoices in a batch but the time per transaction is per invoice. It will be important to track the number of invoices processed rather than the number of batches to obtain accurate ROI metrics.

In addition, some possible KPIs you may want to track are:

- Internal for RPA CoE Use
    - ◊ BA
        - ➤ Average throughput time for PDDs
        - ➤ # PDDs/BA/month
    - ◊ Developers
        - ➤ Average throughput time for automations
        - ➤ Average throughput time per developer
        - ➤ # Automations/developer/month
        - ➤ Change order (CO) frequency and reason (COs may be required each time a change is made to an automation in production, and multiple COs may indicate a need to improve testing and code review.)
- External to management

- ◊ # Automations in production
- ◊ Annual hours saved
- ◊ # of Departments helped with automations
- ◊ Annual dollars saved
- ◊ ROI

- System/platform change management
  - ◊ Advance notice of change per platform, i.e., mainframe change notice one week prior to impact
  - ◊ # of automations impacted by platform change

Also, determine the type of analytics and metrics that your software program provides. It may be necessary to design your automations in a way that the software itself can capture the metrics.

Continued Stakeholder Involvement

It's very important to have the continued support and input of your stakeholders. Their input will be invaluable to the integrity, stability, and growth of your program. Here are some of the areas that should be included from a highly regulated banking perspective, though your industry may not require all these or may require others:

- IT security
- IT infrastructure
- SOX

- Risk
- Compliance
- Audit
- Business continuity

Make a list of your stakeholders. Meet with them and ask if they know of other stakeholders who should be included. Time spent making sure all stakeholders are involved regularly will greatly help with change management and decrease resistance. Don't just go full steam ahead and automate, then let your stakeholders find out when the automation goes into production. This may make them angry and feel slighted as they were not involved.

Include them as early in the process as feasible and don't just include them. Listen to them! Improve your policies and procedures and best practices by listening to them. They are experts in their areas and if you work with them and listen to them, your product will be even better.

Do not just produce and throw over the fence at them. They will not like it and although it may be quicker in the short run, it will cause delays and lack of trust in the long run.

So many interesting points of view come out of these inclusive calls. You may add additional stakeholders to seek input from information obtained on your initial calls.

Your program will grow and continuously improve as a result.

Citizen Developers

Another opportunity for growth of RPA usage in your enterprise is to utilize Citizen Developers. As mentioned earlier, Citizen Developers are employees who do not reside in the RPA CoE. Their primary role in the enterprise is something other than RPA. Due to this, they know their processes very well. If they are both interested and have aptitude with new platforms, they can become an invaluable resource as well as automation advocates in their departments.

For them to develop automations, they will have to be provided the software and receive training. Most RPA platforms offer free online training to facilitate this.

Your policies and procedures for Citizen Developers will be different from those for the RPA CoE. You will want to be able to provide as much freedom as possible for low-risk automations to achieve optimal results. At the same time, you will need policies and procedures in place for Citizen Developers for automations that have higher risk.

a. Risk Classification

One way to approach Citizen Developer policies and procedures is to begin with a risk classification that determines the risk associated with the automation. You may want to start with three basic risk classifications as follows:

- Low
    - ◊ Does not post financial transactions
    - ◊ Does not provision accesses
    - ◊ Only used within the Citizen Developer's department
- Medium
    - ◊ The same but the deliverable is utilized by another department so could have downstream impact
- High
    - ◊ Posts financial transactions
    - ◊ Provisions accesses
    - ◊ Will be run unattended and monitored by RPA CoE

b. *Citizen Developer Policies and Procedures*

You will need to decide how your Citizen Developers will be monitored and managed. If you are in a financial industry or highly regulated industry, you may want to consider having your Citizen Developers work within a development environment and only migrating to production after proper reviews, approvals, and change management has occurred.

One way to achieve this is to set up Citizen Developers on virtual machines and use active directory service accounts for them during development. Only development or QA accesses should be provisioned to help ensure unintended production impact during development. Upon completion and proper review and approvals, the automation can then be migrated to production and made available on production machines.

COLLABORATION: IT INFRASTRUCTURE AND CHANGE NOTIFICATION

As your program matures and touches more systems, you may find that those using the systems are not always notified of system changes looming on the horizon that could impact automations. If you experience mergers or acquisition, you will want to be particularly astute and proactive to try and identify possible system/platform changes to be best prepared for them.

Typically during mergers, SMEs meet regularly to decide on the system/platform that will be retained in the Go to Model (GTM). They will also make plans for migrating from the current system(s)/platform(s) to the ones chosen for the GTM. Get to know who will be meeting regarding the systems/platforms that your automations use and stay in regular contact with them.

Do not rely on word of mouth that is possibly three points removed. You may get partial or inaccurate information, or even sheer gossip.

Ask questions. Are there multiple modules of the platform used at your company? Are all the modules being replaced or just select ones?

Document them somewhere. Yes, in Excel if needed. You can have so much information about so many areas coming at you so quickly that it can become confusing. If needed, create Visio process maps to visualize the interaction of systems and represent the current and GTM for the platforms.

It is advisable to meet with IT on a regular basis separate from your other stakeholder meetings to discuss the new automations in your pipeline as well as those that are existing in production. These meetings can be even more beneficial than simple awareness of upcoming system changes. IT can also be helpful in pointing out areas where stability and efficiency could possibly be improved such as connections to databases or application programming interfaces (APIs). Using these types of interfaces can eliminate or decrease user interface interaction and screen scrapes, which are inherently unstable and prone to problems with system/platform version upgrades.

It's also important that you or a member of your team attend IT meetings where upcoming changes are discussed. If your enterprise is of significant size, you are going to continuously encounter new systems/platforms and acronyms as your programs grows. You will never know it all. You will be venturing into areas that are not your area of expertise. If your area of expertise is on the business side, the technology language and acronyms will be challenging. If your area of expertise is on the technology side, the business language and acronyms will be challenging.

When I first started in RPA, I was also attending the Harvard Business Analytics Program (HBAP). As part of the program, we met weekly via Zoom for live classes and in smaller groups weekly for discussions. I was very comfortable with discussing the business side and implications but when the discussions were surrounding the technology, I would typically say "IT is not my area of expertise." In one of these meetings, a HBAP colleague challenged me.

"Laura," he said, "can you name one business that is not heavily impacted by technology?" I thought about it for a minute and responded: "No, I cannot." He responded, "Then you need to make technology one of your areas of expertise."

I told him I didn't know where to start. There were so many acronyms and terminology I didn't understand that it was overwhelming. He told me he experienced the same thing when he transitioned into the business side from IT.

He said to take one acronym or topic at a time, Google it, and watch YouTube videos until I understood that one, then move to another. Of all the valuable takeaways I gained from HBAP, that absolutely was one of the most valuable. It was so simple but a much-needed wake-up call and attitude adjustment. I put this into practice every day and am continuously learning. I no longer say "IT is not my area of expertise." I suppose I was using that as a cop-out in a way. It sure let me off the hook in putting in the effort to learn.

No more cop-outs! I encourage you to do the same. Whether it's business acronyms, technology acronyms, or new areas in your industry, don't cop-out that it's not an area of expertise for you. Ask questions, search, and learn.

All expertise started out this way. No one was born with this knowledge. They had to acquire it little by little and so can you. Also, surround yourself with people who will challenge you as they will help you grow and improve your skills and your capabilities as well as your success.

IMPORTANCE OF COMMUNICATION

There are so many moving parts involved in automations running successfully. It's important to make sure that anything controllable is controlled. An area of particular importance to note in your organization is how changes to policies and systems within your organization are communicated.

- When changes occur to policies or systems, are they proactively communicated?
- If so, how are they communicated?
- Is it effective or is there so much communicated at one time that the stakeholders can't possibly decipher quickly what applies to them?

Ask your IT SMEs how this communication is handled. You may be surprised by the response. It may range from not knowing what you are talking about to "We don't do any communication. Employees know that the change impacts them when something breaks."

If you're among the fortunate, then your organization has a well-thought-through plan of communication. Users of systems or stakeholders of policies are effectively identified, and proactive communication is required and monitored. Anonymous internal customer surveys are conducted regularly and gaps in communication are identified. Plans are made to improve, and follow-up metrics are obtained to ensure that improvements are made.

Can you expect this? No, most likely not. Don't expect this to be the case for your organization. If it is, that's great but it's best to expect the unexpected until you know for sure about the quality and timeliness of communication.

Lack of communication can be frustrating, Prior history with certain departments or people may lead you to want to knee jerk when communication is inadequate but *don't*. Call them or set up a meeting to discuss and don't start out by letting them have it out of frustration. Instead, start on a positive note. Something like "I understand ... and I want to see if we can discuss possible options."

Do not start out combative and frustrated or you will get a combat. It is important to lead being the keel, i.e., stabilizing and reacting calmly to unexpected occurrences. All leaders, if they're being honest, will tell you that at times being the steadying keel is challenging. Be honest with yourself and learn how to get back to being the keel during those times.

Have you made that transition? If you continue down this path of RPA and continuous process improvement, at some point you will need to decide whether you want to transition to a leader who is the calm in the storm.

I must be honest and say there are still times when I want others above me to take care of the hard stuff, i.e., just make them do right. But I must calmly fight that. My primary role as a leader is to make sure that the programs and initiatives, I lead are successful, those above me are successful, those below me are successful, and other employees are successful. The more you can manage and deal with issues and progress helping ensure success independently without being needy to management above, the more valuable you will become to them.

If you're an individual contributor in RPA or process improvement, you can go ahead and improve your value to your team and manager by proactively facing the challenges that come your way, sharing them with your manager, always thinking through the possible solutions, and striving to have solution options to present at the same time as the issues. This will show your ability to take responsibility and develop solutions — not just hand off problems to management. This is an invaluable skill to work on for your team, other employees, and management. In addition, responding calmly may save you from unnecessary indigestion and sleepless nights. So, know the facts before responding/reacting to issues or challenges.

Of course, it's very challenging not to respond emotionally in some cases — especially if you are tired, wrung out, and fielding issues coming one after another. You're not perfect and neither are others but for your own sake and others, try your best to not knee jerk. Take a breather. Literally, when you feel like the veins on your forehead or your eyes may be about to pop out of your head, breath. That's right. Calm yourself down. Take a minute to step back and breathe deeply before responding.

Use the breath 6-7-8 method. Breathe in through your nose to the count of 6, hold it for 7, then breathe out through your mouth for 8. If you practice this, you can even do it while sitting face to face with others and they'll never know you're doing it.

Another key factor in being a great leader is being trustworthy. If your team comes to you with challenges and frustration, listen intently and strive to help them overcome the challenges. That is your job as a leader.

I have been privileged to report to some fabulous examples of leadership. As I reflect on what makes or made them great leaders, I noticed that they listen well without taking the devil's advocate view. They truly try to understand your viewpoint and determine how they can help. They understand that their purpose is to help knock down barriers to success not to convince you that the barriers aren't there or that you should deal with them yourself.

To help enable your leader to be the best manager they can be, you should write challenges down clearly defining them, step back and determine what would be helpful for your manager to do to enable you to deal with them before you discuss challenges with your manager. Then, clearly state to your manager what the challenges are and what you think the manager can do to assist. Ask yourself whether you are asking your manager to do something you can or should do yourself prior to approaching them.

Also know what you are going to do and how you are going to respond if your manager is non-responsive or combative when you make your request. Stay calm and professional. At the same time, clearly know your boundaries. Is this a situation where it is appropriate to be firm and say clearly "This is a barrier to success and not one I can remove. It needs upper-level support and involvement?"

Sometimes, the less said, the better. You don't want to engage in a back-and-forth argument with your management. If your views are so different that your manager will not listen, it may be time to seek a different position. In fact, it may be best for you and for them.

If you get to this point, continue to be extremely calm and professional. If you are frustrated, don't show it. Take a walk. Step back from it and don't re-engage until you can approach it unemotionally.

Even then, you may be better off deciding what you want to do to move on professionally. How can you deal with the current situation unemotionally? How would you like to leave the situation? Don't leave it in a mess as some sort of revenge. That will only solidify their stance that they're better off without you.

If you proceed calmly, you may see them turn around and come back with a more placid, helpful attitude. If not, by continuing to do your very best for your employer while you're there, you will earn respect and not burn bridges. It is essential to your own integrity to do everything you possibly can while in the employment of others to make their initiatives successful even if you are not in total agreement. You may find that unfortunately your way may not always be the best way. Listen!

Try not to be a victim though of the grass is always greener on the other side syndrome. You will have challenges in any role or position. If you are fortunate enough to be in positions that there are many different people contributing, there will inevitably be differing viewpoints. If you can adapt and accept this, you may find staying in your current role may provide the opportunity for you to learn from others that have views differing from yours creating superior results.

GROWTH AND STRATEGIC PLANNING

At one point, I was challenged to roll out 300 automations within a year. I worked with my team to develop a plan to accomplish this and what would be required. I presented it to management complete with the resource requirements and a scheduled roll-out calendar.

Ultimately after seeing what would be required in black and white, management decided to move toward ROI, customer experience improvements, and employee experience improvements goals. Confession: I was *so* thankful. With the previous goal based on the number of automations, we would have been focused on targeting automations that were the quickest to develop and get to production. I knew ultimately that stakeholders would probably say "So what? What have 300 automations done for us? Have they saved us money, increased capacity, improved customer, or employee experience?"

If you are in upper level of management, be careful about your goals. Are they truly driving the results you want to be measured by? Does the number of automations really matter to your stakeholders or are they more concerned about efficiency improvements and savings as well as customer and employee experience improvements?

As I said, I was thankful our goals changed as I was not in agreement with the initial goals. However, I was fully committed to doing the best job I could for management.

If they had stuck to the original 300 automations in a year goal, I was fully prepared to give it my all and move full steam ahead to achieve their goal and achieve it well.

How you handle these types of challenges is a personal decision you must make. There are limits to what I can personally support. If the requests don't violate ethical, moral, or legal boundaries, I can continue to give it my all and be supportive.

There have been times in various roles through my career that I couldn't fully get on board with strategic, tactical goals or the manner they were being addressed although there were not ethical, moral, or legal violations. I just couldn't get inspired initially to give it my all. In these cases, do yourself and everyone else a favor — either get on board with the plans and give it your all or move on! Otherwise, you are a ball and chain around management and peers' legs. You may think that your true thoughts and feelings aren't known, and they may not be, but your attitude and underlying beliefs will shine through and be problematic. If you can make that leap to give it your all, both you and your enterprise will benefit as you both support them and you learn the value of listening to the viewpoints of others broadening your own knowledge.

Decision time. Can you give it your all and do your best to make the initiative successful? If not, you are doing more harm than good to yourself and your enterprise.

TRANSITIONS AND CHANGE

This brings me to the topic of transition and change. As I said earlier, change is inevitable. Whether you work for yourself or a big corporation, nothing stays the same forever. Our world is continuously changing, and every second is different from the previous second. Most of us resist change. It's stressful. Take someone out of their routine and you will most likely see stress.

Car keys aren't where they should be. Stress. Standard morning routine interrupted. Stress. Thought process interrupted. Stress. Day's schedule turned upside down. Stress. You get the picture. Even those of us who thrive on continuous process improvement don't like change that is imposed upon us and particularly if it is unexpected.

Can those of us who are into change management prevent change or control it even in our own lives? No, we cannot. Of all the groups of people in the world, change should not come as a surprise to us or throw us off, but it does, and it can.

So, how can we best prepare ourselves and our teams for change? My most recent positions have been with large enterprises. As enterprises grow, autonomy and control of personal decision-making tends to diminish. Inevitably, bureaucratic policies and procedures will come into play even for those enterprises that embrace an entrepreneurial culture. Do they not ultimately develop policies and procedures regarding expenses, etc. or do they really allow those with entrepreneurial spirits to spend money and invest freely on whatever they dream up to be a winner idea? Isn't there a limit even to the biggest pots of gold or does everyone just continue to run around and spend at free will without regulation?

Hopefully, you get my point. Even the self-employed should have self-guidance in place. You should be continuously aware of the cost and benefit of your efforts and make prudent decisions. If you work for an enterprise, be proactive in treating the money like it's your own.

With this thoughtfulness in mind, you will inevitably need to control expenses and manage productivity. Many people resist being controlled. There are people who like being controlled and find peace and serenity in being told what to do and how to do it. I refer to this type of personality as a "plow horse." They are content doing the same thing every day for years and doing what they are told. They are very uncomfortable with change and not typically proactive to figure out how something should be done. They have great value for enterprises as we need plow horses.

Then there are personalities that are always questioning the status quo. "How can things be better? We have met this goal. What's our next goal? Let's move it." I call these "racehorses." Racehorses are rarely content for long doing the same thing over and over. They are continuously seeking out new challenges.

Do you know what you are? Are you a racehorse or are you a plow horse? The sooner you can determine what your personality type is and what type work you feel most comfortable doing or thrive in, the sooner you can get yourself into an opportunity where you are more likely to thrive long term. We can force ourselves to perform and perform well outside our interests and personality but ultimately performing by sheer willpower may cause you to burn out. Also, you may find yourself continuously spending time dreaming of a way out or into a position that is more within your comfort zone.

If you struggle to identify what makes you tick or what makes you happy, consider hiring a coach. If you don't have the funds to hire a coach, reach out to those at work who you admire and trust and ask them for their input. But for this input to be worthwhile, it's essential that you can be transparent with them.

If the person you're considering as a coach is someone you feel you must put on your happy face for and act like you love everything, they aren't the right person to turn to for guidance. For this reason, it's often necessary to go outside your current workplace. Daydream for a minute. When you are dreaming about a better position for you, a better life, what does it look like? Write it down. Now, where can you identify people who are in those positions?

LinkedIn, Facebook? What about books? Are there any books written on those topics?

Start trying to learn more about your "dream" situation. You may indeed be suffering from the "grass is greener on the other side" syndrome. You can save yourself a lot of pain and time by doing some research to truly understand what it would be like in that day-to-day existence.

If you desire more freedom in your work, it may come at the expense of having a regular dependable paycheck. Or maybe not. If you want freedom and a regular dependable paycheck, that's good to know about yourself. Seek out positions or companies where you can have both, if possible.

If you are okay with not having a dependable paycheck, how long is that realistic for? If you really want that lifestyle, start planning. Write down your plan and have specific goals. Just because you dream of something doesn't make it magically happen.

I have dreamed for decades of writing a book. I didn't know what kind of book or what the book would be about but just dreamed of writing a book. It wasn't until I narrowed my dream down to what kind of book and developed a timeline and goals to achieve that I began to get on the road to turning my dream into reality. I first set my goal for completing the first draft. Then I determined how many words it would be, created a spreadsheet, decided what time of day was best, and set aside 30 minutes early in the morning before the demands of the day started distracting me. I set an alarm on my phone for 30 minutes and was diligent about respecting this time — well when I could, to be honest. Actually, my day job got in the way much of the time and writing this book took much longer than originally planned.

But I tracked my progress in a spreadsheet documenting start time, time spend writing, words written that day, total words written, and a column that calculated percent complete. As I progressed, I added a "Woohoo!" Woohoo! 10% complete. 20%, 30% … This gave me a visual accounting of my progress. At 1–2 % gain per day, I steadily made progress toward my end goal while working a very demanding full-time job.

Interestingly, my time spent writing every morning made me even more efficient at my job. Issues became clearer. Tracking progress and aligning enterprise strategic goals to tactical goals and monthly, weekly, and daily goals became more solidified.

But what does all this about knowing yourself better and aligning your innate interests and energy with what you do every day have to do with growth and strategic planning? The time you spend thinking about what is not to your liking is time that could be spent producing and planning growth and strategy where you are for you and your team.

It is much better for you and those on your team for you to be honest with yourself and work toward finding your calling sooner rather than later. You may have excelled at managing areas that are stable and rarely change where your days have been relatively predictable. Upper management noted how you thrived as a manager and put you in this new area. But now you are miserable. You long to be back in an area where your days and challenges are more predictable. You long to be back in a place where issues are predictable and consistent, and you know exactly how to manage them.

If so, get back to one of those areas. Both RPA and/or continuous process improvement are changing environments by their nature. Note how I don't just refer to process improvement — I say "continuous" process improvement" as the cycle never ends. If you are in the beginning stages of considering RPA and/or continuous process improvement as a career, you must not only embrace this fact but thrive in this type of environment.

Hopefully, this has started your process of doing a bit of introspection on yourself. If you're still with me, you have most likely determined at least that you're not totally averse to facing constant change and/or challenges daily in your work. Now, where in the world of RPA or continuous process improvement, is your best fit?

Even managers need to make this decision, and seasoned high-level managers at the executive level need to be aware that RPA and continuous process improvement can shake the foundation you have built your career upon. You will need to become even more comfortable with having your thought patterns, decision-making methods, and daily, weekly, and monthly routines changed. This is very difficult, more so for some than others. Do you come from a strong IT background? If so, then you are going to have to realize that RPA is not like the traditional developing you have done for decades.

I once interviewed for an RPA executive position at a very well-known Fortune 500 company. The position would be to stand up their RPA Center of Excellence (CoE). During the first interview, the interviewer told me how the interview process worked at the company with multiple interviews and panels. No problem there. The turning point for me, however, came when she asked me what language I wanted to present my whiteboard session to the panel in. Even though I knew she was referencing programming languages, my first thought for my response was, "English." I asked her to clarify, which she did saying "Java or C#."

I knew the corporation was headed down an extremely difficult path. They believed that RPA development was the same as system development. I graciously thanked them for the opportunity to move on in the interview process and said I wouldn't be a good fit. It's up to you how much time you want to spend educating and helping change long held views internally.

As you develop the strategic plans for your programs, whether you know you are in the right position for your personality and strengths and weaknesses, you owe it to your enterprise to continuously keep in mind and have plans for succession planning — not just for your position but for all the positions on your team. Currently, there is high demand for these skill sets and much competition and recruiting to fill positions. Make sure you have a plan in place and can adjust quickly to changes in your staffing.

Also, be aware that there may be higher turnover than you like with contractors. This causes lost time onboarding and training new contractors so they can perform optimally. Make sure you have basic models in place that include documentation to make handoffs easier. Are your PDDs, code storage, code reviews, UATs, and monitoring standardized? Do you have in place reviews to ensure compliance to standards?

The larger your programs become, the more essential these factors will be. As soon as you have one area standardized and running smoothly, you may experience slippage in others. Incorporate not only policies and procedures but also reviews and audits to ensure the policies and procedures are being followed. When the cat's away, the mice will play.

Having succession plans is invaluable for you and your team. As the pandemic has shown us, our working environment can change in an instant and not always by our choosing. We indeed owe the enterprises that provide us these opportunities plans to provide business continuity and stability should we or other team members be absent.

CONCLUSION

THERE ARE SO MANY aspects of LEAN continuous process improvement and RPA programs. The endless cycle of learning and change can be exhilarating and challenging and at the same time a bit daunting. I hope that you enjoy your journey in this exciting space as I have enjoyed mine.

My wish is that this book has helped you start, stabilize, and grow your programs. I would love to hear from you about your challenges and your successes. I have had the benefit of others sharing with me along this path. This book is my way of giving back to others.

Now that you are on this journey, I hope we will meet again often to share experiences and build our enterprises, our experience, our methods, and our improvements. If we are driven by relentless curiosity and an unbounded desire to learn, we will never cease in providing continued benefit and efficiency improvements, doing more with less.

Please share your experiences by emailing me lhendrix@theleanmission.com.

Until I hear from you or better yet meet you in person, I sincerely wish you the blessings expressed in the old Irish blessing below.

May the road rise up to meet you.
May the wind be always at your back.
May the sun shine warm upon your face.
The rains fall soft upon your fields and until we meet again,
May God hold you in the palm of His hand.

Wishing the very best to all of you in your efforts!

Laura

APPENDIX

FREQUENTLY ASKED QUESTIONS

1. What have been your biggest challenges and what advice would you give others to help avoid or deal with these challenges?

For LEAN process improvement, the biggest challenges I have faced and continue to face are resistance to change and the tendency for some people to be unwilling to listen to the opinions and ideas of others. These tendencies are a part of human nature and will not change.

Training in team dynamics, facilitation, and LEAN and six sigma methodologies will help you immensely when you face these challenges. Training and experience will help you focus on the process, not the people — and anticipate, work through, and overcome inevitable challenges and resistance to change. Most of the time, even the staunchest of opponents will begin to see the value of changes made. In some cases, those who resist the most may become your biggest champions. They can be very beneficial in assisting others through the discomfort of change by sharing their experiences.

For RPA, the biggest challenges have been due to fear of losing jobs and misunderstanding regarding how automations work. Employees are afraid their jobs will be replaced by bots. This can happen so is a valid fear and needs to be addressed. It is helpful if you can help ensure that those whose jobs you automate are not laid off. Who is going to share with you how to automate their process if it means they are going to lose their jobs?

Another challenge faced for RPA programs is the misconception that bots could just go and do whatever they want and wreak havoc. This is untrue. Robots are like the wheels on a car. They go where the steering wheel tells them to. Can you imagine driving down the road and turning left but suddenly your car speeds up and turns right instead? So instead of ending up in Miami, FL, you suddenly find yourself in Anchorage, Alaska.

There may be people on the earth who have tried to get others to believe ludicrous stories like this. This is the stuff of science fiction. Cars don't take off, at least today, on their own making their own decisions where they are going to go. Neither do bots. Bots are very obedient. They do as they are told.

In addition, bots don't operate in grey areas like humans do. Humans may think something is close enough to what they were told and decide to execute even though it isn't exactly as they were told. Bots don't do this. They do what they are told, period. If the conditions aren't what they are told, they throw an error or are handled as exceptions and even then, they are told what to do based on certain criteria.

Another challenge is IT believing that automations are the same as developing systems and treating them the same. Automation development is not the same as system development. Automation development does not change underlying systems or platforms — they use systems and platforms the same way humans do.

Try your best to help IT understand this. Plan on possibly having a lot of resistance initially. Be patient yet persistent.

2. Is senior leadership support essential? What are critical elements to understand for senior leadership?

Senior leadership support for both LEAN process improvement and RPA programs is imperative to success. I personally would not even consider taking on standing up these type programs without senior leadership support. These programs have so much innate resistance from employees that it is imperative that you have senior leadership support to get past the resistance.

For senior leadership to support your programs, they need to understand them conceptually and they also need to be shown their value regularly through dashboards and KPIs.

If your enterprise does not proclaim "LEAN" thinking and actions as a mission to eliminate waste, your efforts and results will be limited. Also, another fact to keep in mind when working toward ensuring the maximum potential of achieving optimal efficiency with automation and continuous process improvement is that "continuous" is vital. If your enterprise is not continuously striving to improve, it will be continuously falling behind. As the quote by Sam Waterson states, "If you're not moving forward, you're falling back."

As soon as we make an improvement, we must keep in mind that there already is a better way. Keep moving forward. Keep questioning and being curious. How can we do it better? Don't settle. Make this a mission, your mission and your team's mission.

Just deciding this is your mission and your team's mission is not enough. It is critical that this mission is coming from the highest rank of your enterprise — your CEO. It's also important that your team is tasked to help achieve this goal and this is clearly communicated throughout the enterprise. If you do not have this level of clearly communicated support, you are wasting your time and your team will become frustrated.

Let's assume that you have determined that you have the level of support needed in your enterprise. Now what? You need to have a focus. A great way to start is to document your executive's strategic goals, then align your team's mission to the strategic goals. Once you have your mission aligned to the strategic goals, it's very important to break down the team's mission and strategic goals into tactical goals.

What is this? Tactical goals are those achievable tasks that your team can do in a time-based manner to lead to a successful mission for both your team and your enterprise. This book provides practical guidance to you in a systematic way to identify your goals, work toward them, and monitor success.

Yes! Success! No one wants to start on a mission that is not successful. Arm yourself with all the knowledge you can to help ensure success. Being a leader of change is difficult. There will be many naysayers who will challenge your efforts. It will be important to your success to stay positive. Count and celebrate your achievements. Try to get to know others who have been successful in change initiatives and surround yourself with them.

It is very exciting to see the many benefits that LEAN missions provide to enterprises and individuals. Focus on the benefits and envision success. What will it look like for you and your team? Be specific.

3. How do you communicate your value to your leadership team?

For my programs, I look at the total economic impact of the results. It is imperative to focus on results, not actions. Actions are not synonymous with results. Make sure you don't focus on how much work you and your team are doing. Focus on the results.

To take a total economic view of your results, you will need to track and provide metrics for the following categories:

1. **ROI** – (Hours saved * cost/hour)/cost

2. **Capacity creation** – How much can your transaction volume be increased before you experience incremental expense? How much will that incremental expense cost compared to what it would cost if the process isn't improved or automated?

3. **Customer experience improvement** – This is subjective and can be difficult to monetize. Some people use Net Promoter Scores (NPS) but there are many factors that go into improvements in NPS so this would be a hard sale. This may need to be provided at a more subjective level reported either by customers or employees who work closely with employees.

4. **Employee experience improvement** – This can be a challenging category as well to measure. However, if possible, include process improvement and/or

automation related questions on your employee surveys.

5. **Error prevention** – This is an important category as errors cost time, money, and result in negative brand perception. If there are tracked error rates with the process you are improving or automating, measuring improvements is easier. However, much of the time, the processes may be manual and difficult to track errors. If you are addressing processes that have fees and penalties associated with errors, you can track fees and penalties before and after improvement or automation.

4. **What are some challenges people may face improving processes?**

Management Support

For process improvement, you will often encounter resistance to change. As stated previously, it's imperative to have upper-level management support to be able to push past this resistance and be successful. With upper-level management support, you can push past the resistance and accomplish phenomenal improvements

There will inevitably come a time when you hit the wall. An initiative you are working on will need more resources than your company can or will provide. That decision by management won't sit well with you. You know what the process improvement will do for the company. You have worked for months with a team and have come up with the solution only to be told no. It isn't important enough to be prioritized at this time.

I once worked on a process improvement to address a broken process that resulted in 5–7 escalated customer complaints per week. I assembled a team of stakeholders and we determined that there would need to be more provisioning of IT resources to address. We weren't provisioned those resources. I was told since this had been an ongoing problem for years and it was only 5–7 customers per week, it wouldn't be prioritized.

Being mathematical, that didn't sit well with me. 5–7 complaints per week amounted to 260–364 per year or 2,600–3,640 every 10 years. What would have been the value of those customers every year? You must also count all the friends, coworkers, and family those unsatisfied customers would impact and help turn toward competitors.

So now what? You already knew there was value in pursuing the improvement or you wouldn't have worked for months on it. What does this example prove? That there is still value in the improvement. And? Until you have upper level backing to obtain the resources to achieve the improvement, you are wasting your time. You are wasting your time thinking about it, stewing about it, and talking about it. Save your breath to cool your coffee!

Table it and move on. What next? Proactively take your mind from dwelling on it forcefully. What other opportunities for improvements do you have? Decide which ones you need to focus on and when your mind wanders back to stew upon your disappointment, guide it gently but firmly to other opportunities. If it helps, set a reminder on your calendar in the future to revisit the opportunity — and when your mind wants to not let go of it, remind yourself you will review it on the set date on your calendar to see if circumstances have changed. Until then, focus on other opportunities.

What if management is not supportive of you or *any* of your improvements? If that is the case, it may indeed be time to move on. How did you get into a situation like that in the first place as a professional whose expertise is process improvement? Seriously spend some time answering that question.

Could you have seen signs that you were not going to be supported? What were those signs? Write them down. Did they show up before you took the position or only afterwards? Could there have been a way to detect them before? If so, write them down. Make sure you keep those in mind as you search out your next path. Even with the best screening, we all find ourselves in positions at times that did not live up to how they were touted or to our expectations.

There will be disappointments in any position. The better you become at managing those disappointments quickly, the more energy you will have to concentrate on productivity and moving forward. Get over it and move on! Even if you stay, move on from trying to change something you have absolutely no hope of being successful doing and spend your time on the things you can change and where you can be successful.

There is a rule known as the cost of quality called the $1, $10, $100 rule. Basically, the rule states that it costs $1 to prevent a problem, $10 to correct the problem once noticed internally, and $100 to correct it once noticed by the customer. If management at your enterprise does not understand this ultimate concept of the need to support process improvement, it's highly unlikely that they will be grow as their quality will take them backwards faster than they can make up for it.

Gaining Executive Support

It's essential to first be sure that you have valid, measurable examples of opportunities, cost, and benefits for your programs — whether continuous process improvement or RPA. Make sure that the management of the primary stakeholders involved are fully committed to support your efforts to gain executive support.

Create your presentation incorporating metrics for Return on Investment (ROI) that respected SMEs within the enterprise will help confirm are valid. Reach out to those SMEs and tell them what you're thinking and ask for their advice. Listen to them.

Be sure you do not overestimate ROI. The executives will be reviewing closely the actual ROI compared to the ROI you originally present. You will quickly lose credibility and future support if you overstate ROI.

The Wolves Knocking at your Door

When your program becomes highly successful, you may face different challenges. In the story of the big bad wolf and the three little pigs, the wolves are outside the houses. Let's talk about the wolves inside your house. Yes, those competing to get ahead internally who will be focused on their own ascent in the organization. There are several means to grow and rise through organizations. Unfortunately, there are and always will be those within an organization who have a win-lose mentality.

To them, there is a set amount of success — a limited quantity. They can't rise in the organization if they don't take something from someone else and so instead of focusing on win-win where they create and grow their own value, they focus on stealing yours.

Let me tell you a story about the golden retrievers my husband had before we got married. Their names were Sheba and Fred. Now Bill loved to take Sheba and Fred to the park where he would throw tennis balls in the lake and Fred and Sheba would retrieve them. He would throw the tennis ball way out into the lake and Fred would scramble and swim ferociously, grab the ball and head back to shore.

Sheba would stand on the bank and when Fred got close to the bank, Sheba would jump in, swim to Fred, and hold him under water until he let go of the ball. She would grab the ball, swim to the bank, and take it proudly to Bill. Bill first recounted this story to me as justification of why he said women are smarter than men. Not my belief — just Bill's from observing Fred and Sheba — but I do love it.

I have experienced human Shebas in my life, repeatedly. There can be thousands of balls in the lake that need to be retrieved but they don't focus on any of the balls that aren't being retrieved. They see you almost to the bank with yours and they want to take it. Getting the glory and credit the easy way. Really, folks? If they are successfully able to do this, in the end, the truth will be known. It may take a long time but eventually it will come out on them.

If you have people try to, or succeed in, stealing your ideas and achievements, don't under any circumstances let them steal your drive for pursuing your goals! They can steal momentarily but don't ever let them steal your drive. Let it go and move on to the next challenge and enjoy it.

5. What are some challenges that people may face with RPA?

For RPA as the number of automations in production increase, the time spent monitoring and troubleshooting increases — taking more time and focus away from new automations. At about 40 automations in production, you will most likely start seeing that you need additional resources for monitoring and level 1 troubleshooting to make sure your team's resources can continue to produce.

You will also need an automated means for incident reporting, assigning, communication, and SLA tracking. Consider creating a form and SharePoint workflow for submitting incidents and notifying parties of the incident, status, and resolution of incidents. This solution will provide improved efficiency for your team, and improved communication to stakeholders.

As I write this, the world of RPA is in a very strong growth mode. The demand for experienced employees far exceeds the supply. You and your employees will most likely receive regular solicitations for other job openings. No matter how good you are to your employees, how supportive or how much you pay them, other businesses may offer them more and they may leave.

Be prepared and have a plan in place for how you will address the vacancies left by departures at all levels. Are these roles that you can have contractors fill until permanent staff are onboarded? If you have a proper plan in place, your program will not suffer delays due to staffing changes and will keep progressing rapidly forward, providing the lift and efficiency improvements needed. Don't be blindsided.

If you ever find yourself in the position that key employees leave, assess your current state quickly and adapt. Some steps that are helpful are as follows:

1. Obtain a list of must dos from managers. Also, have them list "nice to do but not required."

2. Discuss back-up plans for every current employee. How would you respond if everyone walked out? How would you maintain? Not being Chicken Little with the sky is falling here, but just recognizing that the demand in the industry might cause continuous changes in staffing. This ultimately helps ensure a very resilient model and plan and is invaluable.

3. Focus on stably maintaining automations in production, i.e., monitoring and troubleshooting.

4. Make a list of the process improvements that are in process and need to stay in process. Decide whether to start new process improvement initiatives until staff is replenished. Which ones can be put either on autopilot or holding pattern?

Be open with upper management about the challenges and stresses on your team by making a list of current challenges and your proposed plan for dealing with the challenges. With a clear and well-thought-through plan, and an added huge dose of reality check, you will successfully negotiate these minefields. You will be prepared, and your programs and teams will be much better for the time spent planning.

6. What additional advice would you give others who are either starting into process improvement and RPA or would like to improve their programs?

Continuously reflect on your own programs and how you can improve them. Take a dose of your own medicine and use process improvement tools on your own programs.

A gap analysis is very useful for planning and identifying where you want to be, where you are, and the gap between the two states. Once the gap is identified, it's easier to take each component in the gap and develop a plan to address each one and its priority.

Work with your teams methodically on this. Meet regularly with your managers once a month and review the improvement goals you have set for the year, the status of the goals, the next steps, timeframes, and ownership needed to achieve it.

Once a year, review your current goals and establish your improvement goals for the coming year. Start the conversations by determining what the new vision is. Seek input and add new goals and tasks.

Ask your team the following questions:

1. In a perfect world, what would our programs look like?
2. In what areas do you think we are performing well and why?
3. What areas do you think we need to improve?
4. What steps are needed to improve them? (Break these down to specific tasks that are achievable in the coming year, then set a timeframe and ownership for the next steps.)

It is helpful for your team to have a visual that shows them clearly their completed achievements - turn the tasks green when complete and provide visual confirmation of progress.

If you have ever experienced annual goal setting that is not looked at and reviewed until the next year, you have probably experienced the realization that at least some of the goals were forgotten and not achieved during the year. The constant review and task assignment throughout the year by meeting monthly to review will make you much more likely to meet your goals.

By performing a gap analysis, it should be clearer where the gaps are between where you want to be, where you are, and what needs to be done to get from A to B. However, you will need to further drill down to make the analysis and subsequent plans more attainable.

Break down each of the large goals into accomplishable tasks. By doing this, the tasks become clearer and more realistic to achieve. Working on the smaller tasks needed to achieve the larger goals provides immediate gratification and a feeling of accomplishment as the individual tasks are marked complete.

The following are examples gaps identified by gap analyses for a process improvement program and an RPA program.

Process Improvement Program Current:

- Quality team charter documenting the process improvement for every initiative not regularly maintained
    - ◊ Some initiatives missing initial charter
- Tracker not maintained after every meeting
    - ◊ Touch bases every two weeks to ensure momentum not lost — no tracking of this and last update on tracker

Process Improvement Program Future:

- Quality team charter for every initiative regularly maintained
- Tracker maintained after every meeting

◊ Touch bases every two weeks to ensure momentum not lost — tracking of this and last update on tracker

Process Improvement Program Gap:

- Quality team charter missing initial charters and not regularly maintained
    - ◊ Need to oversee to help ensure charters are created and maintained
- Tracker not maintained after every meeting
    - ◊ Need ability to track updates and deficits on tracker — should be updated for every initiative every two weeks to maintain momentum

In conducting gap analysis this way, the gaps become better defined and can be addressed more systematically. It is then helpful to break down the gaps to specific tasks required to meet goals and establish ownership and time goals.

Gap Name	Description	Task	Owner	Time Goal
Quality team charters	Quality team charter missing initial charters and not regularly maintained	Identify missing charters and create	Laura	April 5
Tracker maintenance	Tracker not maintained after every meeting	Add this to Power BI dashboard (Manager view)	Manager 1	March 29

An example for a gap analysis for an RPA program is as follows:

RPA Program Current:

- Power BI dashboard source file not populated
- Organized software and license upgrade program not fully documented and planned for annual upgrades
- Development and review not standardized
    - ◊ Automated review not followed and no plan
- Throughput not standardized and efficient
    - ◊ Not standardized
    - ◊ No consistent use of reusable modules
    - ◊ No tracking of compliance to standardization and use of reusable modules
- Inefficient production monitoring
    - ◊ Monitoring not centralized and standardized
- All automations not using official audit log modules for proper audit log
- Accesses to platforms very manual and time consuming for both initial provisioning and review
    - ◊ "Sandbox" accesses containing all accesses for specific user groups not created (These would contain needed accesses for specific user groups

and eliminate the need to request each access individually.)
- ◊ BA "sandbox" security group not created
- ◊ Developer "sandbox" security group created but not populated or used

RPA Program Future:

- Power BI dashboard complete
- Organized software upgrade program
- Standardized development and review
    - ◊ Automated review as much as possible
- Improved throughput
    - ◊ Standardization
    - ◊ Continuous improvement and use of reusable modules
    - ◊ Tracking
- Efficient, centralized production monitoring
- Use of reusable modules optimized
- Sandbox accesses
    - ◊ BA
    - ◊ Developer

RPA Program Gap:

- Power BI dashboard source file needs populating

- Software upgrade plans need finalizing — robot upgrades — attended and unattended
- Development and review need standardizing
  ◊ Need plan for utilizing automated review — studio review and checklist
- Need monitoring of throughput time
  ◊ Need standardization of development
  ◊ Need consistent use of reusable modules
  ◊ Need tracking of compliance to standardization
  ◊ Need tracking of use of reusable modules
- Need efficient, centralized production monitoring
- Need to increase use of reusable modules
- Sandbox accesses
  ◊ Need to create and use BA and developer sandbox security groups

Here is an example of the breakdown of gaps identified into specific tasks required to meet goals and establishing ownership and time goals:

Gap Name	Description	Plan	Owner	Time Goal
Power BI dashboard	Source spreadsheet needs populating	**Populate spreadsheet** Tasks: Complete spreadsheet) – highlight yellow all incomplete cells and make list • Rework dashboard to completed timesheet • Switch to real time dashboard updates	• Complete spreadsheet (Laura) • Rework dashboard to completed timesheet (manager 1) • Switch to real time dashboard updates (manager 1)	March 24
Sandbox access — BAs	Need to create and populate BA security group	Create security group for BA access, have ID management populate with accesses	Laura	April 12
Robot upgrade plan not created	Need attended robot upgrade plan	Create plan	Manager 3	April 19
Checklist use	Need to habitualize checklist use	Track use of checklist for review and improve usage	Manager 2/manager 3	April 26
Reusable modules	Need tracking of use of reusable modules	Start with official audit generic automation use, make list of all automations and which ones use generic modules and which do not	Manager 2/developers	May 3

Sandbox access — Developers	Need to populate developer security group	Determine accesses needed for sandbox and create	Laura/manager 2	May 10
Automated code review	Need to customize software capabilities and use	Customize review module	Solution architect/manager 2/manager 3	May 17
Development standard	Need standardization of development	Create standards and best practices for development parameters vs. config files, etc.	Laura/manager 2/manager 3	May 31

7. How do you keep enthusiasm for process improvement and RPA programs at a high level so the programs don't start declining and die?

It's very important to have a regularly updated and communicated dashboard/presentation that clearly states the ROI provided by your programs. I include bar charts and other graphics that clearly show the ever-increasing savings provided by my programs. Management loves these charts as they provide the metrics clearly.

8. There is so much to do it is overwhelming. Where do I start?

Take some time right now and make a list of areas where you need to make headway. List the specific goals you want to achieve and break them down into achievable tasks. Set specific time deadlines for achieving the tasks. Regularly work toward being able to check off items on the to do list as complete. If you or your team cannot achieve your initial tasks, break down your tasks to smaller tasks. It's very important for everyone involved to be able to see progress.

Don't wait until the entire elephant has been eaten. Break it down into bites and start checking the bites off one at a time. That way, you and your team won't become so overwhelmed, and they will be able to see their achievements.

Depending on the maturity of your programs, your list might look like this:

- Identify opportunities
    - ◊ Identify departments to be reviewed for opportunities
    - ◊ Prioritize and assign responsibility for identifying opportunities
        - ➤ Document plan for opportunity identification
        - ➤ Document prioritization
- Gain executive support if not already in place
    - ◊ Provide metrics and list of opportunities
- Standardization
    - ◊ Process improvement program

- ➤ Regular quality team (QT) meetings
- ➤ Regular spreadsheet updates
- ➤ Notes
  - * In OneNote
  - * Contain:
    - – Basic meeting minutes
    - – Next steps section (also to be used for agenda for next meeting)
- ◊ RPA
  - ➤ PDDs, PDD review
  - ➤ Logging, log design review
  - ➤ Separation of Duties (SOD)
    - * Documentation
    - * Orchestrator role finalization and review
- Perform gap analyses
  - ◊ Process improvement
  - ◊ RPA

MANAGING RESISTANCE TO CHANGE

Who likes to change? Well, probably the first answer that comes to mind is the people who are deciding what the change will be, not the people being asked/forced to change. Keeping that in mind, is it no wonder that most people don't like those who represent, ask for, or demand change?

And that is you. Yes, you. You are the one coming to them and telling them that their process needs to change. In their minds, you are telling them "Your baby is ugly." And they hear it as "Your baby is UGLY!" You are the big, bad wolf.

They take it personally. Then what? They blame you and many times; they don't like you. They like the way they are doing things. Otherwise, they would change it themselves. They are comfortable. This is how they have done this for years/decades. Who are you to come in and tell them they need to change it? Well, you are either the one who recognized that processes must be improved for the enterprise/business to survive, or the one management has put in that role.

Let's get back to the big bad wolf. The big bad wolf first goes to the house owned by the three little pigs. It's made of straw and the wolf quickly blows the house down. Next, the three little pigs build a house of sticks. The wolf huffs and puffs and blows the house down. Then, the three little pigs build a house of brick, and the wolf can't blow it down. Still being determined to destroy the house, the wolf climbs the chimney to enter the house and falls into a pot of boiling water. The pigs are safe.

Where many people will view you as the big bad wolf trying to blow their house down with your changes, you are not. You are the one providing the guidance they need — telling them they need a stronger house and how to build it. Their competitors are the big bad wolf trying to blow their house down and destroy them.

Remind them if they will listen. They may not listen so don't be surprised. This is why you need management support. If properly supporting you, management will clearly communicate their desires and goals for these changes and improvements. If your management says they support you but don't provide this level of communication to others, you will be continuously fighting an uphill battle. You may want to let go of that battle and choose projects, if possible, where management will provide more clear communication and support.

Others may never like you, but you are not here to win a popularity contest or make friends. You are here to make a positive difference and help the enterprise be as competitive as possible. If the enterprise fails to be competitive and fails, they won't like you then either. However, it is very important to be respectful to others and try to understand the difficulty they have with thinking outside the box. Do not take it personally.

Something I have seen through my experiences leading change is that there are those who in the end understand and even though reluctant to make changes end up being champions of your efforts. It is knowing this that can help you get through the difficult times. Don't fight them constantly. Listen to their concerns and do your best to address those concerns. In doing so, you may earn their respect and develop a better solution.

Understand that their reluctance to your suggestions is not about you at all. They may be afraid of losing their jobs, security, and the ability to support themselves and/or their families.

Is this a sobering thought? Your efforts could cause others to eventually lose their jobs. It's very important to keep reminding yourself that the world is continuously changing. It's not your responsibility to ensure that other people do their best to keep up with change, so they don't become obsolete. However, whenever you get an opportunity, help others you are working with seize opportunities to learn and develop new skills. They may not even seem willing to do this.

One of the most combative, reluctant employees I have ever worked with became a big proponent of process improvement and automation. She went from resisting the automation when we were originally discussing improving and automating her process to embracing it and becoming very knowledgeable about the technology. If we ran into issues with her automation, she eventually became as adept as anyone on the CoE team in troubleshooting. When we suggested possible causes, she would say "I have already tried that." Love it!

The definition of continuous is "without cessation." Don't expect the resistance to change to stop. If you do want it to stop, you may not be in the right field. It is very important to not just expect and tolerate the prospect of the challenges that come with improving efficiency but to love it. To know deep down somewhere that at the end of the struggles is improvement that will benefit everyone involved and that is not a negative.

Companies and people that do not change become obsolete. Which is the better choice for you and your enterprise: pushing change to be competitive or standing by and allowing your company and their employees to become obsolete?

If you are still reading this, you probably are already committed to achieve the improvements that will be required for your enterprise to be competitive and survive in a quickly changing world. Welcome aboard for this amazing journey! If you have already spent time in this field and achieved efficiency improvements through change, focus on the good that has come from your efforts.

Share these benefits with others that are struggling to promote change or accept change.

What next? Where do you start? It's overwhelming, isn't it? If you're looking at changes needed every way you turn in your business, try not to be overwhelmed. Start by making a list.

Be positive. By making your lists, prioritizing, and improving one step at a time, you will make progress. Even if it seems extremely slow, it is nonetheless progress. Your enterprise will be further along in this continuum of improving efficiency than if you threw up your hands and gave up.

Don't give up! No matter how challenging it is and what obstacles you face, if others have put their faith in you to accomplish changes and improvements, keep moving. Keep trying to gain ground even when it's one baby step at a time and especially during those times when you seem to take one step forward and two steps back.

If you don't persevere, how will these necessary improvements happen? With as many challenges as you are facing, it's highly unlikely that they will just happen on their own, isn't it? What good are you to anyone at your present company or in future roles if you just give up?

If you aren't currently in a position where you have been tasked with process improvement for others, you can still improve processes — your own. Focus on your part of the process, which is what you have control over. When I first started doing process improvement, that is what I did.

RESISTANCE TO STANDARDIZATION

The employees or managers who resist standardization, efforts to develop policies and procedures, and efforts to enforce them may come as a big surprise to you. It certainly has been to me at times in my career. Some of the employees you think will be supportive turn out to be resistant and some you think will be resistant are supportive.

You may experience this in meetings to discuss policies and procedures and enforcement. The resistant parties will at times be relatively quiet and not participate much in the discussions. They believe that they are hiding their resistance, but their silence speaks volumes. Then there are resistors who are extremely vocal. These people may be easier to address. Listen to them. Their concerns are valid and should be addressed. Don't ignore them. They will not go away on their own.

You can't force people to like change, but it is certainly advisable to be aware of those who are not going along with the flow. Ultimately, they may be quietly seeking other positions. You cannot stop this and may not want to. They may be a ball and chain around the enterprise's ankles as you try to make improvements.

If you have employees on your team who are quiet when discussing change, have in mind a succession plan for them. You may not need it but it's best to have a succession plan in place, so you aren't thrown totally off your game if they suddenly give notice.

Although it's not preferable to lose good people, if they don't like increased standardization and policies and procedures that are vital to process improvement and efficiency, it's most likely best for everyone if they leave. To have your programs running optimally, standardization is paramount as you scale. Remember that processes left on their own, like nature, will tend toward chaos.

The larger an organization becomes; the more important standardization becomes. Although leaders try to do their best to reduce the negative impact of standardization and policies and procedures, there will always be some employees who resist change and standardization. Imagine the difference between having 5 employees doing things their own way and 100s or even 1000s doing things their own way.

Resistance to change and standardization will particularly be evident during or after mergers and acquisitions, particularly if one side of the merger/acquisition loses its original identity and must conform to another's identity, systems, policies, and procedures, etc. However, even with that in mind, we should always try to learn from these changes. Can something be changed in the future to minimize the negative feelings brought on by change while still making necessary changes to adapt to new leadership?

If you are a manager tasked with ensuring that the necessary changes happen for your new leadership to reach their strategic goals, it's not within your power or in your or your team's best interests to capitulate to those who resist. The bottom line is that your new leadership will be held to task to meet their goals, and these goals will roll down to your team. If you don't make sure your team does their part, you and your team may be replaced by those who can.

You will absolutely be doing your team and employees no favors by being so nice that your leaders' strategic goals aren't met. In fact, it's best that your team not only helps them meet their goals but helps them *surpass* them.

There may be times when even your very best efforts to find a win-win are met with such resistance that it will turn into crazy making for you. No matter how you put something, no matter how you try to listen and understand, the person on the other side of the discussion will have a win-lose mentality and will hang on to it so firmly that you will need to decide: do I continue to do the same thing over and over again expecting different results? The reported definition of insanity. Or do I accept that there is in impasse and move on?

There are several factors to keep in mind when deciding to cease and desist your efforts to negotiate with them. Will your management be supportive if you put your efforts on hold due to the resistance? If you don't know, the best way to find out is to ask them. If management wants you to continue, do they understand the time it is taking and the projects that will be delayed while you and your team continue to try to gain cooperation?

Your management doesn't have a crystal ball any more than you do. Be very clear about the projects that are being put on hold while your team tries to deal with difficult people. This exercise to clearly lay out the cost of dealing with the difficult person(s) will not only help your management make decisions, but it will also help you understand and be able to articulate the true cost.

REFERENCE TOOLS AND RESOURCES

TEMPLATES

Initial template for tracking opportunities for process improvement and/or RPA:

PRIORITY (HIGH/ MEDIUM/ LOW)	PROCESS NAME	DESCRIPTION	LEAN WASTE TYPE	VOLUME (HIGH/ LOW)	PROCESS IMPROVEMENT OPPORTUNITY (YES/NO)	AUTOMATION OPPORTUNITY (YES/NO)	COMMENTS
High	Posting Tickets	Tickets are posted throughout the business day using paper tickets. The initiating employee writes a paper ticket, and a manager must approve. The ticket is then walked to another employee who processes the ticket by entering it into the system. The processed tickets are then taken to another employee who files the processed ticket.	Manual, Repetitive, Motion, Printing, Waiting	High	Yes	Yes	Are approvals actually needed prior to processing or can levels be set that do not require approvals? Manual processing needs to be eliminated via RPA.

LEAN MISSION

Template for tracking process improvement and RPA opportunities separately:

Opportunity #	Division	Department	Process Name	Contact(s)	Added By	Date Added	Process Description	Status	Volume (Annual)	Time (Minutes/Transaction)	Hours Savings (Annual)	Cost/Hour	$Savings/Year	Comments
1														
2														
3														

For the spreadsheet for process improvements using DMAIC, the status dropdown options may be as shown here:

- Opportunity Identified
- Define
- Measure
- Analyze
- Improve
- Control
- Not Pursued (There are some that you identify that upon further study you will choose not to pursue)

For the spreadsheet for automation opportunities, the status dropdown options may be as shown below:

- Opportunity Identified
- Assess
- Process Definition Document (PDD)
- Development
- Production
- Not Pursued

Solution Selection Template:

	Weight	OPTION 1	OPTION 1 (Weighted)	OPTION 2	OPTION 2 (Weighted)	OPTION 3	OPTION 3 (Weighted)
Improvement in processing time	4	6	24	3	12	10	40
Error improvement	5	1	5	8	40	3	15
Employee experience improvement	1	1	1	5	5	1	1
Customer experience improvement	3	9	27	10	30	10	30
Total score			57		87		86

Implementation Plan:

Action	Responsible Party or Parties	Due Date	Status	Comments

Communication Plan:

Who will deliver? (Person)	Who is the target audience? (People)	Who is responsible coordination? (Person(s))	What will be communicated? (Text) (Can be linked to a separate Word document)	When will it be communicated and how often? (Date/time)	How will it be delivered? (Platform)	Status	Comments
Carol Speaks — Communication Dept.	Call Center Employees	Team Facilitator, Team Communications Lead, Call Center Manager	"On October 15, 2021, a new process will be implemented......"	Oct. 1 10:00 AM CT, Oct. 7 10:00 AM CT	Email		

Training Plan:

Who will develop and deliver? (Person)	Who is the target audience? (People)	Who is responsible coordination? (Person (s))	What will be required for training? (Text)	When will it need to be implemented and how often? (Date/time)	How will it be delivered? (Platform)	Status	Comments
Tommy Trainer	Call Center	Team Facilitator and Call Center Manager	On-demand video and Job Aid	On or before Oct. 1 – on-demand indefinitely	Company training platform		

Monitoring and Control Plan:

Key Performance Indicator (KPI)	Reporting Responsible Party	Reporting Frequency	Distribution Mode	Recipients	Action Items
% Calls Processed Successfully (# Successful/# Total) Goal = 95%	Joe Smith	1 X/ week by COB each Friday	Email	Todd Jenkins, Call Center, and Fred Smith, Solution Architect	Todd and Fred to review root cause Pareto chart to determine whether additional improvements can be made. Periodically review goal and increase when needed.

Pilot Plan:

Who? Pilot Participants	What?	When?	Where?	How?	Responsible Parties
Susie Smith's Call Center team – Carol Jones, Betty Walker, Tom White, Allen Carlisle	Team to use solution for all calls	1/15 – 1/22	In their standard locations	Team to be provisioned access to automation pilot	Fred Smith, Solution Architect, and Susie Smith, Call Center Manager

Transition Plan:

Transitions to Who?	What?	When?	How?	Responsible Parties
Betty Clark – Director, Call Center Operations	Metric reporting and monitoring	3/1	Paul Tutor on Betty's team to report metrics weekly to Betty	Paul Tutor and Betty Clark

Orchestrator/"Control Tower" Roles

Additional columns may include Queues, Triggers, Processes etc.

TEAM ROLE NAME	ASSETS			PACKAGES			ROBOTS		
	Create	Modify	Delete	Create	Modify	Delete	Create	Modify	Delete
Administrator									
CoE lead									
Code migration agent									
Business analyst (BA)									
Developer manager									
Developer									
Production monitoring									

RPA Logging/Database Maintenance Plan:

LOG LOCATION	PLAN	INTERVAL	RESPONSIBLE PARTY (IES)
Example: unattended machines	Change default parameter in config file to limit local storage	Continuous	RPA CoE - John Smith
Example: database	Delete/archive files over 30 days old	Weekly (Automated script run)	Database team (point of contact = Don Brown)

User Acceptance Testing (UAT):

Automation Name:		Conducted By:	
UAT Date:		Pass/Fail:	

STEP	Description	Expected Outcome	Pass/Fail	Comment	Screenshot

Transition Plan:

Transitions to Who?	What?	When?	How?	Responsible Parties
Betty Clark – Director, Call Center Operations	Metric reporting and monitoring	3/1	Paul Tutor on Betty's team to report metrics weekly to Betty	Paul Tutor and Betty Clark

Orchestrator/"Control Tower" Roles

Additional columns may include Queues, Triggers, Processes etc.

TEAM ROLE NAME	ASSETS			PACKAGES			ROBOTS		
	Create	Modify	Delete	Create	Modify	Delete	Create	Modify	Delete
Administrator									
CoE lead									
Code migration agent									
Business analyst (BA)									
Developer manager									
Developer									
Production monitoring									

RPA Logging/Database Maintenance Plan:

LOG LOCATION	PLAN	INTERVAL	RESPONSIBLE PARTY (IES)
Example: unattended machines	Change default parameter in config file to limit local storage	Continuous	RPA CoE - John Smith
Example: database	Delete/archive files over 30 days old	Weekly (Automated script run)	Database team (point of contact = Don Brown)

User Acceptance Testing (UAT):

Automation Name:				Conducted By:	
UAT Date:				Pass/Fail:	

STEP	Description	Expected Outcome	Pass/Fail	Comment	Screenshot

Gap Analysis Tracking and Addressing for Programs:

GAP	PLAN	RESPONSIBLE PARTY	TARGET DATE	MILESTONE CHECKPOINTS
Synchronized automated updates	Review and develop plan for consolidating/synchronizing opportunity identification portal, RPA tracker and metric reporting	Laura	Plan due — July	Monthly — during team strategic planning meetings — put on monthly strategic planning agenda
Complete historical metrics	Obtain volumes and time per transaction for existing automations	Laura	Friday, 4/16	Every day
Libraries not utilized as much as possible	Review and determine what additional automated steps can be included as a reusable library	Developer manager	May	
Share drive accesses	Determine best way to restrict accesses	Technology manager	May	
Metric capture	Are metrics being consistently updated in master list?	Laura/managers	May	

RESOURCES

Links for additional resources can be found at www.theleanmission.com.